REVIVAL –
Before and After

Paul H. Moore

ISBN-13: 978-1508477785
ISBN-10: 1508477787

DEDICATION

This work is dedicated to those who long for revival!
May God grant vision and encouragement to those who pray.

All Scripture quotations are taken from the
New King James Version of the Bible, unless otherwise noted.

CONTENTS

FOREWORD

This book is actually Paul's thesis for his Masters in Ministry from International Seminary, written in 1990. If that seems like ancient history – it is. (Literally, the work spans several centuries. ☺) However, it's just as valid today as the day it was written, or maybe more so…

Our nation is in deep need of a visitation from God. Without going into great detail, this study points out the conditions before and after some landmark revivals. Even if you just skim these pages, it will become obvious: We are ripe!

Paul has walked with the Lord for forty-four years and has been a student of revival just about as long. Since he wrote this paper, he has not ceased to pray earnestly and fervently for God to come and do what He has done before. He is consumed with our need for God to revive the Church and save the lost. Paul knows that there is no hope apart from the Lord's intervention, and that compels him to intercede and encourage others to do likewise.

One of two things will happen: Either we will have revival in our lifetime – or die praying for it. Either Paul will be like Abraham, who didn't get the city he sought because of God's timing – or he will be like Simeon, who could die in peace, seeing the salvation of the Lord. (Hebrews 11:3, Luke 2:29-30) Either way, in the fullness of time, God will come. Whether it is in our lifetime or not, God will answer Paul's prayers and reward his efforts.

The question is this: Will you join him? Will you pray? If you are praying, will you press in and persevere?

It is our prayer that publishing this work will encourage those who are of a like heart and calling – to the glory of the One who revives.

Myrna Moore
Valentine's Day 2015

INTRODUCTION

Throughout history, man has experienced both times of spiritual prosperity and barrenness. In fact, decline and decay seem to be as much a part of our spirituality as they are a part of our moral and physical make-up. Perhaps this is why Arthur Wallace defines revival as "rain from heaven."[1] Rain is necessary for the preservation of life. As a lack of rain brings a drought, resulting eventually in famine and death, so a lack of God's personal involvement and manifest presence in the Church produces spiritual drought and barrenness.

Over the years, revivals have seemed to counteract seasons of dryness by restoring the reality of God's power and glory to His people. God's people, in turn, are to be the "salt of the earth" and the "light of the world," preserving it and destroying the darkness. (Matthew 5:13-16) When the Church is not functioning as it should, we are all in trouble!

Seen in this light, the study of revival becomes very important. It is through the sudden, explosive intervention of God that the Church (and, perhaps, all of mankind) is spared from self-destruction. Therefore, I will attempt to explore this important phenomenon. To do so effectively, we need to understand a pattern we seem to have inherited from our forefathers of the faith.

As we study Israel's history, it soon becomes apparent that they repeatedly failed to keep God's word. Walking with God, they would be blessed; disobedient, they would be cursed, ushering in a season of spiritual decay. Each time, however, God – in His infinite love and mercy – would raise up a prophet or judge to remind them of the

1

covenant. Repenting, the blessing would be restored, but not for long. Sin inevitably would follow, and a roller coaster pattern of blessing and cursing was formed.

Similarly, the history of the Church has seemed to duplicate the Old Testament pattern. Since seasons of spiritual decadence seem to be followed by times of renewal, it would appear as if revival plays a key role in counteracting our propensity for sin.[2] Sin separates us from God, and, as it accumulates and infects a nation, judgment ensues. (Isaiah 59:1-15) It seems that it is in these times of utter darkness that God's infinite mercy brings revival to His people. (Isaiah 59:15-21) Therefore, this work will attempt to elaborate upon and interpret the preconditions of revival in light of our history and God's love for us.

Revival has also been said to restore the saints to "normal Christianity."[3]   Simply put, this means that God uses revival to get us "back on track." While this seems to be true, however, it is not complete. Revivals have also seemed to restore spiritual momentum to God's people. In times of spiritual decline, the forward progress of the Church grinds to a halt. Revivals have rekindled zeal and service, producing great forward progress and reform – not only in religion, but also in every other aspect of society.

Dr. F.B. Meyer once observed that "there has never been a great religious revival without social and political reforms."[4] Slavery, child labor and severe and extreme working conditions have been greatly altered as a byproduct of revival. Organizations such as the Y.M.C.A., Salvation Army, numerous missionary societies and a host of other charitable and educational groups have been formed as the result of the mighty outpourings of God's Spirit. Therefore, I will also study and comment upon the changes in society brought about by the revivals considered in this study.

Following a section on the nature and need of revival ("What is Revival?"), we will focus upon the conditions prior to, during and following five major moves of God's Spirit. They are: The Reformation in Germany and Switzerland, the First Great Awakening in America and in England (the Wesleyan Revival), the Great Revival, the Prayer Meeting Revival and the Welsh Revival. Following a consideration of these phenomena, I will give my observations, insights and prescriptions in the "Conclusion."

While there are other movements of God's Spirit that could be included (such as the Latter Rain or Jesus Movements later in this century), I am confining my study to the five cited above. It would take at least a dissertation to do justice to this subject. At least, this is a start...

WHAT IS REVIVAL?

Before we can study the effects of revival, we must first define our terms. Winkey Pratney, author and lecturer, tells of an informal survey he has used to determine the extent of his audience's knowledge of the subject. Often, he would ask the following questions:

"How many of you know we need revival?"
(Almost everyone would raise their hand in agreement.)

"How many of you want a revival?"
(Again the vast majority would agree.)

"How many of you know what revival is?"
(Here the numbers would drop off alarmingly.)

"How many of you have ever experienced a true revival?"
(Very few, if any, would respond)[5]

Interestingly enough, according to Gallup,[6] the vast majority of Americans believe we need revival. A Gallop poll conducted in 1980 states that approximately 80% of those surveyed acknowledged our need for revival. Yet, very few can define it!

Webster defines the word `revive' as: 1: the return to consciousness or life 2: to raise from languor, depression or discouragement 3: to raise from a state of neglect or misuse 4: rejuvenate.[7] To revive implies the restoration of life or recovery from a state of apathy or lethargy. Spiritual revival, therefore, would be the act of restoring the life and power of God to an apathetic Church. The word `misuse' in Webster's third definition may even give us a clue as to the cause of that spiritual apathy.

Time and again, Israel fell into severe darkness, because she neglected the counsel of God's Word. In fact, both Israel and the Church have experienced times of great spiritual fervor, as well as times of great spiritual decadence. If God's people are "the light of the world," a lamp to be set on a lamp stand (Matthew 5:14-16), we could say that history reveals times when the lamp was burning brightly and other times when it only produced a faint glow. Though the lamp is consistently supplied with fuel, its wick can cover with carbon and refuse to shine. God is not going to stand idly by, while this happens.

> A bruised reed He will not break, and I smoking flax He will not quench; He will bring forth justice for truth. He will not fail nor be discouraged, till He has established justice in the earth; and the coast lands shall wait for His law. (Isaiah 42:3-4)[8]

No, if the Lord will build His Church (Matthew 16:18, Psalm 127:1) and the Church will fulfill the Great Commission (Matthew 28:18-20), God cannot allow the light to be extinguished.

"Revival," therefore could be defined as God tending the lamp, trimming is wick and fanning the flame. General maintenance demands some attention, but – when the wick is badly charred – He must take drastic measures. The great revivals of history are just such occasions. The ones examined here are indicative of the special times or seasons, when the Lord draws very close to His people, manifests His awesome presence and breathes His breath (Spirit) upon them. Malachi puts it this way:

> Behold, I will send My messenger, and he will prepare the way before Me. And the Lord, whom you seek, will suddenly come to His temple, even the Messenger of the covenant in whom you delight. Behold, He is coming," says the Lord of hosts. But who can endure the day of His coming? And who can stand when He appears? For He is like a refiner's fire and like fullers' soap. He will sit as a refiner and a purifier of silver; He will purify the sons of Levi, and purge them as gold and silver, that they may offer to the Lord an offering in righteousness. (Malachi 3:1-3)

The most concise and, perhaps, the most accurate definition of revival is found in the book of Habakkuk. Burdened by Israel's wickedness and injustice, Habakkuk cries out to God. In Chapter 3, he begins to pray specifically for God to bring revival to the nation, describing a vision of what God is about to do in verse three. Here, he begins with these words: "God came..." As a result, His glory covered the heavens and the earth was full of His praise.

True revival is a visitation of God. It is more than just big meetings and great excitement. It is more than organized mass evangelism. It is more than an emotional extravaganza or "an orgy of emotion," as some sociologists have stated.[9] Revival, according to Richard Owen Roberts is "an extraordinary movement of the Holy Spirit, producing extraordinary results."[10] Revival produces a display of God's holiness and power that goes far beyond any "normal experience."[11]

During times of revival, political agendas, organizational structures and even human leadership is set aside, as the Spirit of God becomes the controlling factor in the Church. Preaching is often replaced by prayer. Excuses for spiritual apathy evaporate quickly in light of the convicting presence of the Holy Spirit. Men's hearts are changed, along with the social attitudes of millions and the destinies of nations.[12] Revival is unlike an human attempt to bring spiritual reform, in that it cannot be confined by state lines, national boundaries, economic classes, racial barriers, educational distinctions, social status or denominational preferences.[13]

Geoffrey R. King, in a booklet entitled "Rend the Heavens," summarized the concept of revival in these words: "Revival is a sovereign act of God upon the Church whereby He intervenes to lift the situation completely out of human hands and works in extraordinary power."[14] Again, Richard Owen Roberts in his book, Revival, tells us that revivals are extraordinary, because of the results they bring.[15] We need these results.

Historically speaking, the Church and society, in general, have proved our need for revival. Often, the Lord has had to move mightily to restore the purity, power and momentum to accomplish His will on the earth. Without revival, the "salt" has repeatedly proven to lose its savor and be "good for nothing but to be thrown out and trampled underfoot by men." (Matthew 5:13) Without the salt's defense against corruption, we would return to the days of Noah, when "the wickedness of man was great on the earth, ... every intent of the thoughts of his heart was only evil continually ... [and] the earth also was corrupt before God." (Genesis 6:5, 11)

Conditions at the time of the bodily return of the Lord Jesus Christ, will also be the same: "But as the days of Noah were, so also will the coming of the Son of Man be." (Matthew 24:37) When the day resembles

Noah's, we need the Lord to come. If He comes by His Spirit, we call it "revival." If He comes bodily, we call it the Apocalypse.

What is "revival?" It is an act of God in which He restores divine life and power to the Church. It is beyond human initiative and control – and, yet, we are invited to participate, as prayer has played a key role in each. Revival transcends the barriers of economics, race, social status, political structures and religious framework. It is the manifest presence of God Almighty. As Owen Murphy says...

When men in the streets are afraid to open their mouths and utter godless words, lest the judgments of God should fall; when sinners, overawed by the Presence of God tremble in the streets and cry for mercy; when, without special meetings and sensational advertising, the Holy Ghost sweeps across cities and towns in Supernatural Power and holds men in the grip of terrifying conviction; when 'every shop becomes a pulpit, every heart an altar, every home a sanctuary' and people walk softly before God – this is Revival![16]

NOTES:

[1] Arthur Wallace, Revival - The Rain from Heaven, title.

[2] Winkey Pratney, Revival, p. 16.

[3] Stephen F. Olford, Lord, Open the Heavens, p. 64.

[4] Richard Owen Roberts, Revival, p. 31.

[5] Winkey Pratney, Revival, p. 14.

[6] George Gallup, Jr., Search for American Faith, Appendix.

[7] Noah Webster, Webster's Third New International Dictionary, p. 1944.

[8] Jesus, of course, also said this of Himself in Matthew 12:20-21.

[9] Richard Owen Roberts, Revival, p. 16.

[10] Ibid, p. 17.

[11] Arthur Wallace, Revival - the Rain from Heaven, p. 15.

[12] Richard Owens Roberts, Revival, p. 21.

[13] Ibid, p. 21.

[14] Stephen F. Olford, Lord, Open the Heavens, p. 15.

[15] Robert Owens Roberts, Revival, p. 23.

[16] Rev. Owen Murphy, "When God Steps Down from Heaven," p. 1.

THE REFORMATION
1517-1560

Though the Reformation lacks the supernatural phenomena usually associated with the great revivals of history, I felt it germane to include. Apart from these cosmic displays, the Reformation follows in the same pattern as the great revivals. After centuries of spiritual darkness and decay, new life emerged, dramatically changing both Church and society. Actually, to deny the sovereign intervention of God through men like Luther, Zwingli, and Calvin would be to deny history itself. Born in an era of exploration, invention, and discovery, the Reformation ushered in a new era in Church history, marked by the revival of spiritual truth.

CONDITIONS PRIOR TO THE REFORMATION

Divine timing and the history of mankind seem to be warp and woof of the same cloth. For example, the Bible says that in the "fullness of time" God sent forth His Son. (Galatians 4:4) Conditions had to be perfect for the event to occur. Nature illustrates this fact each day, as the temperature and barometric pressure coincide perfectly to form dew on the grass. It is in just such a manner that the Lord performs His works in history, also.

For example, by the time of Christ, the world was ready for Him. The "fullness of time" had arrived. Israel had endured four hundred years of silence and spiritual barrenness, causing many to hunger for a new day. The construction of roadways, new methods of communication, and advancement in travel helped to link cities, countries, and even continents for the proclamation of the gospel, and the stage was set for the Messiah. So it was, also, with the dawning of the Reformation. As the Roman Empire played a major part in preparing the world for the arrival of Jesus Christ, in a similar way, major advancements in technology and new discoveries in science and industry helped to prepare the stage for the dawning of the Reformation.

By 1517, the discoveries of Columbus and other explorers ushered in an era of transatlantic exploration. Prior to this time, the ancient world was linked by river systems. Roman Catholicism controlled much of the then known world, with the exception of nations such as England and Holland. Although Roman Catholic countries such as Portugal, France, and Spain led in the exploration and settlement of the Western Hemisphere, it was England that eventually became the dominant influence in the struggle for North America. The opening of the Western Hemisphere played an important part in the expansion of the Protestant Reformation.

Politically speaking, by the end of the medieval times, states had become organized into nations. These nation states, under powerful rulers, developed their own armies and civil service. Often, they opposed the domination of the universal religious rule of the Pope. By the time of the Reformation, many of the nation states were anxious to be free from the control of Rome. Hence, they became supporters of the Reformation.

During the Middle Ages, the economy of Europe was agricultural, and land was the basis of wealth. Exploration sparked trade and commerce, which in turn sparked industry and the rise of a new class of merchants, bankers, and craftsmen. The discovery of raw materials in newly colonized lands ushered in an age of commerce. Middle class merchants began to replace medieval, feudal lords as leaders in society. Trade became international rather than inter-urban. This gave rise to a new economy in which money replaced barter as the primary medium of exchange. In fact, money became so important, that the growing, capitalistic middle class resented sending it to Rome.

Mobility in the social structure was also another change that proved favorable for the Reformation. In Medieval times, one remained in the class into which one was born. If one was the son of a serf, there was little chance to be anything but a serf, except for service in the Church. By the early 1500's, serfdom was fast disappearing and a new, middle class comprised of farmers, country gents, and the merchant class became prominent. This new middle class generally supported the Reformation.[1]

In the Church, itself, a need for reform was also a growing concern among the people. Men like John Wycliffe (1320-1384), John Huss (1369 -1415), and Girolamo Savonarola (1452 -1498) attempted to bring reform by publicly addressing issues of doctrine and practice. They caused quite a stir in parts of Europe with adamant opposition to the Church of Rome. They denounced the authority of the Pope and sought to expose the corruption of Rome.[2] In the end, their efforts only led to their demise. Other attempts to bring reform were sought through the teaching of Erasmus, Thomas à Kempis, and many others. Although they were unable to make much of a dent in the machinery of Rome, they did manage to fuel the fire of dissent across Europe.

By the beginning of the Sixteenth Century, many influential members in the Western Church were crying out for reformation. It was obvious that reform was needed, but what to reform and how to reform were the questions. For example, the Italian bishops felt that the Vatican was top heavy with power, and that the authority of the Cardinals should be diminished. The preaching friars saw the need for personal reform among their congregations to overthrow the increase of evil. The secular lawyers demanded change in the ecclesiastical courts and exemptions that stood as obstacles to effective administration. Very few churchmen, however, saw the need for doctrinal reformation.

No one seemed to think that the Pope's doctrine was erroneous. In the public mind, there was no question that the teachings of the Catholic Church were true. The teachings of the Church were believed to be unaltered through the long centuries of the past and would remain that way throughout eternity. Corruption, politics, power, and authority were considered to be the areas that needed reforming.[3]

Even though many recognized the need for reform, few were willing to do much about it. To demand reform is to denounce abuse. To denounce abuse is to raise doubts in the public mind, to criticize officials and to hold them up to public dishonor. To demand reform would diminish the honor and respect of the Church and only cause further criticism.[4] This type of reasoning paralyzed any efforts of reforming the Church from within. However, ignoring the truth only paves the way for further error. By 1517, the stage was set for an unexpected revolution that would alter the course of history.

THE REFORMATION IN GERMANY

One cannot hear the word `Reformation' without immediately thinking of one man: Martin Luther. Whereas it is true that he was supported and aided by many able friends and followers, even they seem to think that they could not have done the work that Luther did. In more ways than one, he had been chosen and prepared for the mighty task he was to undertake.

As the son of a peasant, he was familiar with the needs and struggles of everyday life. Ordained to the Augustinian order at the age of twenty-four, he entered monastery and began to wrestle with the spiritual doubts and perplexities which seemed to undermine his faith. Later, as a professor and Doctor of Theology, he was drawn to the intense study of the Bible. This was what started it all...

Upon studying the Scriptures, Luther realized that the Medieval Church had lost sight of their teachings. A business trip to Rome in 1511 seemed only to confirm his findings. While there, his visit made a deep impression on his soul. As he observed the religious hypocrisy and the moral corruption of the Papal city, Martin Luther became convinced of the urgent need for reform.[5]

It wasn't, however, until a couple of years later, that Luther experienced a powerful conversion, while studying the book of Romans. For the first time in his life he found peace in his soul through understanding Romans 1:17. Convinced that salvation was through faith alone and not based on a system of merit and good works, Luther developed a system of theology founded upon justification by faith and sola scripture. He realized that salvation was to be had simply by the exercise of faith toward God through Christ – and that the Scriptures were the only authority for anyone seeking salvation.[6]

Though his ideas were revolutionary, Luther never saw himself as a revolutionist. When he first saw the need for reform, he thought his theology could produce it. So, he wrote this to a friend in May of 1517:

My theology – which is St. Augustine's – is getting on, and is dominant in the university. God has done it. Aristotle is going downhill and perhaps will go all the way to hell. Nobody will go hear a lecture unless the lecturer is teaching my theology – which is the theology of the Bible, of St. Augustine, of all true theologians of the Church.[7]

Luther was excited about the progress and impact of his newly found theology, yet he remained deeply concerned with the overall corruption that he saw in the Church.

Not only was the theology of the Church perverted, but so also was the practical outworking of such theology among the people. One such problem had to do with the sale of indulgences. The Roman Catholic Church teaches that penance is the sacrament in which the believer confesses his sin, receives absolution, and performs an act of satisfaction. These acts of satisfaction are known as penance. They are imposed by the priest and are proportionate to the degree of one's sin. The reduction of one's penalty (required penance) by the Church is what is known as "an indulgence."[8]

By Luther's day, the use of indulgences had become a means of financing the expansion of the Church. Pope Leo X had ordered the sale of indulgences to finance the completion of St. Peter's Cathedral in Rome. As first Luther was content to preach against the misuse of indulgences. However, it soon became a different matter when his own parishioners, producing Letters of Indulgences and declaring that they would not put away their sins, objected when he refused them absolution.[9]

Enraged over the issue, Luther wrote a thesis exposing corruption in the sale of indulgences. On the eve of All Saint's Day, October 31, 1517, Luther nailed his "Ninety-five Theses" on the door of the Wittenberg Castle Church. In it, he not only condemned abuses of the indulgence system, but also challenged all comers to a debate. Tens of thousands of copies were circulated throughout Germany, marking the beginning of the Reformation.

Soon sides were drawn and the war escalated. In 1518, Philip Melanchton, a professor of Greek at Wittenberg joined the fight. While Luther was the prophetic voice of the Reformation, Melanchton soon became its theologian. Later in the fall of 1518, Luther was summoned to appear at the Diet (Assembly) of Augsburg, to defend his views to the Church, and the fight was on...

At the Diet, Luther met with Cardinal Cajetan, a representative of the Pope, who demanded that he retract his position. Luther's views were being regarded as an issue of rebellion against the Pope's authority. This could not be tolerated. Luther, however, refused to retract, affirming his first loyalty to the truth. If holding fast to the truth meant an attack upon the Pope, then attack upon the Pope it must be.[10]

In 1520, Luther wrote three pamphlets to be published and issued to the German people. The first publication entitled "The Address to the German Nobility," was aimed at revealing the hierarchy of the Roman Church. The second pamphlet, "On the Freedom of the Christian Man," attacked the theology of Rome by asserting the priesthood of all believers as a result of personal faith in Christ.[11] Later that year, Leo X, after a delay of three years, issued the bull Exserge Domini, which eventually resulted in Luther's excommunication.

The following year, Luther was summoned for an Imperial Diet at Worms to answer for his views. When asked before the Emperor if he would recant, he could only reply, "Unless I am refuted and convicted by testimonies of the Scriptures ... I cannot and will not recant anything ... Here I stand. I can do no other."[12] And the struggle continued... Eventually, the Diets of Speier in 1526 and 1529 and the Peace of Augsburg in 1555 finally granted toleration to Lutheranism in Germany, legally equating it with Roman Catholicism.

Their movement born in doctrinal debate, the Lutherans soon became engrossed in disputing among themselves. By 1580, a document known as the Formula of Concord had to be written and published to settle doctrinal controversies within the Lutheran churches. Lutherans became emphatically concerned with doctrinal correctness, encouraging a strong intellectual emphasis within the Church. Ignoring the more subjective, spiritual aspects of Christianity gave rise to the Pietistic movement of the Seventeenth Century.[13]

THE REFORMATION IN SWITZERLAND

A man of moderation, Luther was criticized for not taking the Reformation far enough. In Switzerland, however, it took a more radical form. In 1519, a brilliant humanist priest at the Church of Zurich came in contact with Luther's theology on justification and had a conversion experience.[14] Immediately thereafter, he began preaching a series of homilies on the gospels, the book of Acts and the Pauline epistles. Ulrich Zwingli (1484-1531) became a prominent leader in the Swiss Reformation, his complete, systematic study of the New Testament laying much of the groundwork.

In January 1523, a Council was held in Zurich to publicly debate the theology of the Reformation. The Catholic Church was represented by a number of clergy, including the bishops from Constance. Zwingli submitted his Sixty-five Theses summarizing his teachings, which he believed were in total harmony with the gospels. The discussion that followed overwhelmingly convinced the Burgomaster and the audience that Zwingli's preaching was completely in tune with the Biblical truth. He won the unanimous support of the town council and his ideas were soon given legal status.[15] The first Reformation Church of Zurich was established on the two major doctrines – justification by faith and *sola scriptura* (by Scripture alone).

During the following three years, under the leadership of Zwingli, the churches in Zurich underwent radical changes. Catholic traditions, images, relics, robes, candles, and etc., were eliminated. Even monks and nuns were permitted to marry, and by 1525 the Mass was completely abolished![16] Zwingli believed that nothing in the worship service should be contrary to the Word of God. His influence made a profound effect upon the Swiss Church.

The Reformation in Switzerland was practically identical in nature to the German Reformation – except for the more radical departure from Catholicism and a hot debate over communion. Luther thought that Zwingli was using rationalism in interpreting the Scriptures on the eucharist. Luther held to the literalness of our Lord's words, "This is My body ... this is My blood." Zwingli, however, held the bread and wine to be merely symbols reminding us of Christ's flesh and blood.

In 1529, the two men met at a conference in Marburg (along with several other prominent Church leaders) to discuss the matter. Although they agreed on all other tenets of the faith, they refused to compromise their positions regarding the nature of the Lord's Supper.[17] Unfortunately, their disagreement over this one issue led to a bitter parting of the ways.

It also gave rise to another form of theology, which eventually became known as the Reformed Faith.[18]

In addition to his work as a reformer, Zwingli considered himself a statesman and sought to solve the problems of Church and State. In his opinion, the Church and State should not function as separate institutions with the State submitted to the Church, but rather the Christian Church should be the Christian State. He believed that ultimate authority resided in the Christian community, not in Rome under the auspices of the Pope. He was a strong adherent to the authority of Scripture and taught that the Christian community was to exercise that authority through an elected civil government. The guidelines of Scripture should govern the affairs of man. Moral offenses should be treated in the same way as criminal offenses – each receiving just punishment. Zwingli's radical ideas may have been too radical for their time.[19]

Another man who played an important role in the Reformation was John Calvin (1509-1564). A French-born, devout Catholic, Calvin converted and adopted the ideas of the Reformation in 1533. He soon began to espouse the teachings of the Reformed Faith, which led to his exile from Paris, France.

Calvin was a second-generation reformer. His was not the work of a prophet, breaking new ground, but rather that of one who systematizes and organizes. If the Reformation was to survive this was desperately needed.[20]

After leaving Paris, he settled in Basel where he completed his greatest work, The Institutes of the Christian Religion. At the mere age of twenty-six, Calvin developed a system of theology that dealt with every doctrine of the evangelical faith. He sought to strengthen original arguments by adding fresh insight and illustrations. He developed an elaborate system of Church government and Church discipline that became widely accepted throughout much of Europe.[21] His work laid the foundation in Reformed theology with its emphases upon the importance of doctrine and the centrality of Jesus Christ. His theology also became the basis of Presbyterianism.

Aside from the theological advancements of the Reformation, Calvin made other contributions that affected the whole of society. For example, he strongly encouraged education. In Geneva, he set up a three level system of education, in which the University of Geneva, founded in

1559, became the top level of academics. His emphasis on education affected America in later years, as the Calvinist Puritans created colleges in the new world.

Calvin also influenced the growth of democracy through his views on governments. He believed that God established the Church and State, and that they should work together to further Christianity. He also believed in a divine call to vocation and emphasized hard work and commitment stimulating capitalism.[22]

THE SPREAD OF THE REFORMATION

The German Reformation not only spread northward into Denmark, Norway, Finland, and Sweden, Lutheranism eventually becoming the state religion of the Scandinavian countries, but also spread southeastern into the Baltic countries. The Swiss Reformation under Zwingli and Calvin spread to the south, east, and west to France, the Netherlands, Belgium, Scotland, Hungary, Spain, and Italy. The road to acceptance, however, was not a smooth one...

Though the French Church flourished to over two thousand congregations by 1560, twenty-two thousand people were slaughtered on August 24, 1574 under the direction of the Catholic Queen Mother, Catherine De Medici. Huguenot blood ran red in the streets of France for the sake of the restoration of the Gospel.

The Spanish Inquisition, led by the Catholic monarch Philip II, sought to crush the Reformation in the Netherlands. Beheadings and burnings at the stake became commonplace, but the Dutch endured and their Reformation succeeded. In Spain and Italy Reformation fires were all but stamped out by the Inquisition under Pope Paul IV. Severe persecution in Hungary was unable to kill the seed of the Gospel, and the Hungarian Presbyterian Church emerged as one of the largest Presbyterian Churches. In time, however, much of Hungary was won back to Catholicism.

Other countries such as southern Germany, Poland, Austria, and Bohemia, though initially set aflame by the Reformation, were eventually won back to Catholicism through repression, bloody slaughter, and the fierce efforts of Ignatius Loyola's Society of Jesus. In fact, the Jesuit priests were the very soul of the counter Reformation.[23]

EFFECTS OF THE REFORMATION

The Reformation was more than a restructuring of the governmental and theological systems of the Church. Politics, economics, education, and religious reforms were also came into being as a result of what the Lord did through the spiritual awakening that began with the German Catholic monk, Martin Luther. At this time, we will briefly consider some of the major political, religious, and educational changes brought about by the Reformation.

Most historians seem to agree that the greatest political changes took place in England. Initially, however, the changes caused by the English Reformation seemed to be for the worse...

Henry VIII tried to pressure Pope Julius II to endorse his second marriage to Anne Boleyn by granting an annulment of his previous marriage to Catherine of Aragon. The grounds: Original sin. Earlier, Catherine had been married to Henry's older brother. When the pope refused to grant the annulment, Henry sided with the Reformers, whom he had earlier opposed. Henry then charged the English clergy with treason for receiving orders from a foreign power. Parliament passed the Act of Submission of the Clergy, placing the clergy of the Church of England under Henry's control.

In May of 1533, the archbishop of England held a court and declared Henry's marriage to Catherine nullified. Henry then married Anne Boleyn, was promptly excommunicated by the Pope in Rome, and all Catholics released from their allegiance to Henry. In November of 1534, Henry responded by having Parliament pass the Act of Supremacy, declaring himself "the only supreme head on earth of the Church of England." By 1540, the crown had abolished all monasteries and confiscated their properties. Henry then sold much of the property to those in his court, creating a new upper class that was to form the foundation for the new Parliamentarianism and Puritanism.[24] Naturally, this new aristocracy opposed any return to Rome. To be anti-Rome, however, did not necessarily ensure a spiritual point of view.

In 1536, the Ten Articles of Religion (drawn from the Lutheran Augsburg Confession) were published, setting forth the basics of the English Reformation. The Scriptures were widely circulated and men everywhere were encouraged to read them and to avoid any practices not taught by them. Then, just three years later in 1539, Henry forced

Parliament to sanction the Six Articles forbidding anyone to teach Protestant doctrines in England, escalating the war on native soil. Eight years later, however, Henry's treason and heresy laws (including the Act of the Six Articles) were repealed under the reign of his son, Edward VI.[25]

For almost one hundred years, the battle between Protestantism and Roman Catholicism continued in England. As various rulers took the throne, advancements and declines of Protestantism issued forth. Many men and women were burned at the stake for opposing Romanism, but, in the end, the seeds of the Reformation took root. The Anglican Church of England, born in 1534 out of political revolution, actually proved to be a step forward in the restoration of Biblical truth.

The Reformation meant the end of control by a universal church. Protestantism replaced Roman Catholicism as the national religion in the lands where it was victorious. The Lutherans dominated Germany and Scandinavia. Switzerland, Scotland, Holland, France, and Hungary gave rise to Calvinism, and the English set up the Anglican Church. The Anabaptists, the only Reformation group to oppose the union of Church and state, became strong in Holland.

Although the Reformation brought about great doctrinal changes, Protestants and Catholics alike accepted the great ecumenical creeds such as the Apostles' Creed, the Nicene Creed, and the Athanasian Creed. They all held the doctrines of the Trinity, the deity and resurrection of Christ, the Bible as God's revelation to man, the fall of man, original sin, and the need of a moral life for every Christian. The Protestants commonly agreed on the doctrine of salvation by faith alone and *sola scriptura* as the only rule of faith and practice, as well as the priesthood of all believers. However, each denomination held its own viewpoint on issues such as baptism, predestination, communion, and requirements for membership.

With the Reformation came a whole new theological system of thought and practice that ushered in the second great period of creedal development. Between 1530 and 1648, many Protestant confessions and creeds were developed, that are still used today in various branches of Protestantism. Justification by faith meant a restoration of the Biblical truth that declares that each man can have a direct relationship with God through Jesus Christ. The doctrine of the priesthood of every believer struck at the heart of the hierarchical system of ecclesiastical mediation between God and man. Sola scripture also counteracted a system of belief that placed decrees, writings, and papal bulls as the final rule of faith and practice.[26]   Truths lost through the ages were being restored to God's people, setting them free from error and bondage!

Indeed, the Reformation was a major step toward the recovery of Biblical truths. Merely recovering them, however, was not enough. If each believer was to interpret God's Word for himself, he must have access to a copy of the Scriptures and develop some skill in reading them. The doctrine of the priesthood of every believer implied the need for literacy, elementary education, and a Bible. Gutenberg and the reformers helped make this possible. With Gutenberg's printing press came a greater ability to distribute the Scriptures, and, considering the establishment of schools as a matter of great importance, the reformers encouraged the development of elementary schools, secondary schools, and universities. Therefore, great advances in education grew out of the movement.

Though the Reformation was making great strides in the recovery of Biblical truths, ending the Spiritual Dark Ages of Christianity and laying the foundation for a new era of spiritual revelation and restoration, it was only the beginning.[27] Jesus spoke of returning for a glorious church, one "without spot or wrinkle or any such thing." (Ephesians 5:27) From our vantage point in history we can see that the Reformation was a first step in the restoration of truth and light. Spurgeon once wrote, "that great religious excitement has occurred apart from Gospel truth we admit; but anything which we as believers in Christ would call a revival of religion has always been attended with clear evangelical instruction upon cardinal points of truth."[28]

Centrally and of more importance than all of the political reforms, religious changes and educational advances brought about by the Reformation, its very backbone was the proclamation of Gospel truths, which the priesthood had withheld from the people.

Men like Luther, Calvin, and Zwingli undoubtedly played an important role in the restoration of truth. Yet, others like Wycliffe, Huss, Savonarola, Erasmus, and à Kempis – equal in valor and boldness – seemed only to fail in their attempts. One thing is sure: Revival is more than the work of men; it is an act of God. The Reformation was more than three zealous men fighting for truth. It was God restoring light in the midst of a dark age.

NOTES

[1] Earle E. Cairns, <u>Christianity Through the Centuries</u>, pp. 227-300.

[2] C.P. Schmitt, <u>Root Out of Dry Ground</u>, p. 78-79.

[3] Owen Chadwick, <u>The Reformation</u>, pp. 11-20.

[4] Ibid., p. 21.

[5] J.A. Babington, <u>Christianity Through the Centuries</u>, p. 314.

[6] Earle E. Cairns, <u>Christianity Through the Centuries</u>, p. 34.

[7] Owen Chadwick, <u>The Reformation</u>, p. 46.

[8] Charles S. Anderson, <u>The Reformation ... Then and Now</u>, p. 23.

[9] J.A. Babington, <u>The Reformation</u>, p. 31.

[10] Owen Chadwick, <u>The Reformation</u>, p. 48.

[11] Kenneth Scott Latourette, <u>A History of Christianity</u>, p. 711.

[12] Charles P. Schmitt, <u>Root Out of a Dry Ground</u>, p. 84.

[13] Earle E. Cairns, Christianity <u>Through the Centuries</u>, p. 320-325.

[14] Ibid., p. 328.

[15] J.A. Babington, <u>The Reformation</u>, p. 45.

[16] Hilaire Belloc, <u>How the Reformation Happened</u>, p. 75.

[17] Owen Chadwick, <u>The Reformation</u>, p. 80.

[18] Earle E. Cairns, <u>Christianity Through the Centuries</u>, p. 333.

[19] J.A. Babington, <u>The Reformation</u>, p. 47-481.

[20] Charles S. Anderson, <u>The Reformation ... Then and Now</u>, p. 44.

[21] J. A. Babington, <u>The Reformation</u>, p. 162-163.

[22] Earle E. Cairns, Christianity <u>Through the Centuries</u>, p. 338-339.

[23] Charles P. Schmitt, <u>Root Out of a Dry Ground</u>, pp. 87-90.

[24] Earle E. Cairns, <u>Christianity Through the Centuries</u>, p. 356-362.

[25] Charles P. Schmitt, <u>Root Out of a Dry Ground</u>, p. 95.

[26] Winkey Pratney, <u>Revival</u>, pp. 43-66.

[27] Earle E. Cairns, <u>Christianity Through the Centuries</u>, p. 386-387.

[28] Winkie Pratney, Revival, p. 58 from C.H. Spurgeon, <u>The Sword and the Trowel</u>, p. 216.

THE FIRST GREAT AWAKENING
1700'S

CONDITIONS PRIOR TO THE FIRST GREAT AWAKENING IN ENGLAND

The Anglican Church was born more out of a political movement than a spiritual awakening. Lacking spiritual leadership, it was dominated by the political leaders of the day. Although the Church in England broke all ecclesiastical ties with Rome, its theology remained practically the same. Changes were gradual and too slow for the common class people of the land.

By 1568, a large group of radicals nicknamed "Puritans," demanded reforms in the Anglican Church. They wanted to "purify" the Church in accordance with the Bible, which they accepted as the infallible rule of faith and practice. They strongly objected to the Romish teaching, practice, and superstition, calling for true ministries of the faith to replace the nominal leadership of the Church.[1] Their reforms were rejected.

Puritanism grew in England and won the support of many lawyers, merchants, and country gentry. However, in 1593, Queen Elizabeth passed a law against them, authorizing imprisonment of any Puritan who refused to attend the Anglican Church. We must remember that the Puritans were not dissenters, as were the Separatists, who demanded separation of Church and State. The Puritans remained in the Church while attempting to bring reform.

During the next fifty years, Puritanism continued to flourish in England, though many grew weary waiting for the Anglican Church to change. Between 1628 and 1640 at least twenty thousand Puritans left England for America in search of religious freedom. Those who remained continued to press for change from within the Church. For a brief period of about twenty years (1642-1662) Puritans even ruled the Parliament. The English, however, quickly tired of their restrictions and recalled Charles II as their ruler. He, in turn, adopted Episcopacy again.

According to Arnold Dallimore's historical account, this violent rejection of Puritanism caused much of the nation to throw off restraint and plunge into godlessness, drunkenness, immorality, and gambling. The Puritans became a thorn in the side of the State Church, continually challenging the ungodly behavior of both the State and the Church. As a result, they faced increasing legal hostilities. In 1662, nearly two thousand ministers, who would not submit to an Act of Uniformity, were ejected from their churches. Forbidden to preach under severe penalty, many were imprisoned, persecuted, and some died.[2]

Concurrently, the philosophy of deism grew in popularity from 1660 1670. This led to rationalism and formalism in religion, as deism doubted everything that could not be rationally proven. The deist believed that God set the universe in order and then left it to its own devices, similar to a watchmaker winding up a watch and letting it run on its own. A deist had one sole responsibility toward God – to acknowledge His existence.

So, deism launched a vigorous attack against the supernatural claims of Scripture. They denied such things as: Predictive prophecies, the virgin birth, the resurrection, and miracles, which they claimed were unproven. Hence, they were determined to demythologize the Bible.

The Enlightenment, having already rejected the idea of moral restraint, welcomed the philosophy of deism. It was the perfect solution to their religious problems. It gave them the security of believing in "God," while substituting a far-away, long-ago, rather harmless "deity" for the God of the Bible, the God of holiness and justice, preached by the Puritans. Furthermore, deism granted a license for sin.

The Church of England did not tolerate the deists. It confronted the deist challenge with intellectual force. Numerous works that apologetically affirmed supernatural aspects of Scripture were written to counteract the heretical teachings. However, this cold, logical, and intellectual defense failed to influence the common people. For the next half century doctrines that had once been considered essential to Christianity were now regarded as open for dispute. As the intellectual war raged on, large numbers of the people fell away, believing Christianity to be false.

Not only did deism produce a spiritual despondency among the people, but it also led to further formalism in religion. Though the English disagreed about many religious issues, they tended to agree on one topic: the rejection of what was called "enthusiasm."[3] Anyone enthusiastic about their faith was considered a "fanatic" and frowned upon by society. Zealous religion in any form was considered a threat to the peace of the empire. Thus, empty formality became the order of the day.

In the wake of formalism a parade of horrors marked the era. A 1689 law prohibiting the importation of liquor "forced" Englishmen to brew their own. So large was the demand, that within a generation every sixth house in London had become a gin shop! Perhaps the worst effects of the "gin craze" were noted by a Church official of the time. "Gin has made the English people what they never were before cruel and inhuman."[4]

The Eighteenth Century also ushered in the industrial revolution, which proved to be another nightmare for the poor.[5] As in the United States, industrialization caused a demographic shift. Large numbers of people came from the countryside to serve in factories, mills, and mines. The working and housing conditions were crude, to say the least. Men and women found themselves in bondage to masters who were relentless and ruthless in their demands. Having no child labor laws, even the youngest children were forced to work in a system that proved to be fatal to many.

The oppression of the poor, coupled with the rejection of moral restraint and indulgence in gin, produced a society of lawlessness and violence. Crime became so rampant that authorities resorted to increased punishment as a deterrent. One hundred and sixty offenses were made punishable by death. One could be sentenced to hang for shoplifting, picking a pocket of one shilling, snatching gathered fruit, snaring a rabbit on a gentleman's estate or even appearing on the high road with a blackened face.[6] Hanging became the gala event of the day as large crowds of men, women and children gathered to view the spectacle. Frequently, ten to fifteen prisoners were executed at the same time to encourage the gathering of crowds. Grandstand seats were sold and gin concessions erected as multitudes gathered for the "hanging shows."[7]

Jail sentences were handed out quite liberally. It was not unusual for many imprisoned for minor offenses to spend a large portion of their lives in prison. Hardened criminals and first time offenders were thrown in together to fight for survival. Since most jailers received no pay, they made a living from bribes, tips, fees, extortion, and the like. Sale of intoxicants, prostitution, and charges for the "release from chains" were among their chief sources of income. Prison conditions were so atrocious during this time (1720-1750) that Twentieth Century researchers have described the period as unparalleled in modern times.[8]

Many efforts were made by various social and religious groups to halt the flood of iniquity throughout England.[9] For example, in 1672 Dr. Anthony Hovneck, a Church of England minister, preached a series of messages called "Awakening Sermons." As a result, small groups of men gathered together weekly to study the Bible, pray, and minister to the poor at their own expense. These meetings became known as Society Rooms. By 1730, nearly one hundred of these Societies existed in London, while perhaps another hundred existed in surrounding cities and towns. The Societies Movement became, in many ways, the cradle of the Revival.

Other attempts were made to help the plight of the poor, sick and oppressed. During the years 1720-1740, many hospitals were established. In 1728 Parliament made a study of England's prisons and presented a report condemning the conditions. However, little was done to change the conditions. In 1736 the Gin Act was passed, prohibiting the trafficking of liquor. Very few supported the new law and it proved impossible to enforce.

According to historian William Lecky, 96 grammar schools were founded in England between 1684 and 1727, yet few parents saw the value of education. Why should they send their children to school, when they could earn a few pence by putting their children to work? Finally, the Society for Promoting Christian Knowledge was formed to provide Christian literature to the common people. Its efforts were highly beneficial and contributed much toward the work of the Revival.

All in all, the successive failures in attempting to better the social conditions of the nation only served to reveal a greater need in the hearts of individuals. Although reforms were desperately needed in every segment of society, social, and religious reform was not the answer. Revival was needed.

CONDITIONS PRIOR TO THE FIRST GREAT AWAKENING IN AMERICA

Across the ocean, the social and moral climate in America was not as depressing as that of England. However, by the second generation of Americans, spiritual and moral decline was indeed clearly visible. In a sermon preached at Boston in 1702, Dr. Increase Mather stated that our fathers came to this part of the world, not to gain worldly advantages, but to seek the kingdom of God. He went on to say that they came to erect a spiritual kingdom for the Lord Jesus Christ to rule and to build churches that would be ordered by the mind of Christ – destined to preach the gospel.[10] And yet, only eighty years later, the glory had departed.

Mather not only spoke of the decline of spiritual fervor in church, but also in the larger society. The civil government no longer operated under the rule and reign of Christ. Iniquity and backsliding were evident everywhere. The Church no longer possessed the power to win converts. Gradually the standards of life and practice were reduced to accommodate the masses.

The first fifty years of colonial life were marked by times of deep moral and spiritual passion. However, by the beginning of the Eighteenth Century, the fires of spiritual fervor had begun to decline. The clear convictions and fiery zeal of the first generation were not evident in their children.

Not having suffered and sacrificed for the freedom to worship, they lacked the same values as their fathers. This vacuum was soon filled by the development of commerce. The increase of wealth gave birth to materialism, further dulling the keen edge of the Protestant witness. Further European immigration followed the flourishing economy, bringing adventurers and released prisoners, men of low morality who had little interest in spiritual matters. All of these factors combined to produce spiritual apostasy in the Church.[11]

In an attempt to counteract the spiritual decline in many New England churches, the famous Half Way Covenant was adopted in the

Massachusetts Colony. Parents who were not church members and had no personal faith were allowed to have their children baptized with the agreement that they would eventually join the church. Often, this proved not to be the case and only added to the general demoralization of the time.[12] Furthermore, many churches adopted a view of the Lord's Supper as a converting ordinance for salvation. In an endeavor to reach the lost, the church opened wide its doors to the unsaved. However, instead of conversion, the Church continued to suffer widespread moral and spiritual decline.

By 1730, Jonathan Edwards, pastor of the church at Northampton, Massachusetts, wrote of the conditions prevalent in his church. Drunkenness, licentious living among the youth and lack of parental control was not uncommon.[13] Pride and irreverent behavior was noted, along with back biting, adultery, covetousness, dishonesty, and – worst of all – a refusal to repent.[14] All of these conditions merely proved to be the darkness before the dawn.

THE GREAT AWAKENING IN AMERICA

Seventeen forty is the usual date assigned by historians to the Great Awakening in America, but by 1734 a stirring had begun in Massachusetts that marked the first tremors of the revival. In an attempt to awaken the people from indifference and complacency, Jonathan Edwards of Northampton, Massachusetts, preached a series of messages. These included topics, such as: Irreverence in God's house, neglect of family prayer, disobedience to parents, quarreling, greediness, sensuality, and the hatred of one's neighbor. According to some historians, Edwards' sermons tended to be deeply theological and too doctrinal and argumentative to make revival history.[15] Nevertheless, God anointed his preaching and several people were remarkably converted.

The entire town was greatly affected by the testimony of one particular woman, who lived a wild, immoral life prior to salvation. As the news of her conversion spread, many others sought a change in life. Edwards reported that over three hundred in a town of eleven hundred, were powerfully converted in half a year.[16] He later described the outbreak of revival as "a surprising work of God."[17]

What surprised Edwards the most was not the intense emotional outburst of the people, but the mercy of a stern and angry God. A large majority of Americans at this time in history were Calvinistic in education and doctrine. They fully believed that they deserved to be "cast into hell" for their refusal to obey God's commands, and yet, God mercifully extended forgiveness and salvation to thousands! (It is estimated that thirty to forty thousand out of a population of one million were converted in the years of 1740-43).

The flickering light that began in Northampton soon spread to other communities in the New England area. New York and New Jersey even experienced spiritual awakenings through the influence of men like T. J. Frelingheyser, Gilbert Tennant, and his bother William. Many powerful preachers (Samuel Blair, John Rowland, Samuel Finley, William Robinson, and others) contributed to the preparation of the Great Awakening. All in all, this was just a foreshadowing of what was to come.

As with every revival or spiritual awakening, a period of decline eventually follows. This was the case in Northampton and the other communities, as well. Opposition arose and controversies developed that hindered the progress of the revival. However, the moral life of the town was much improved and the churches became stronger numerically and spiritually. During the five years prior to 1740, slow but steady progress continued in the colonies as many cried out to God for an even greater move.[18]

It was in the fall of 1739 when a man named George Whitefield arrived in America. British by birth, Whitefield possessed a powerful anointing to preach the Bible. Wherever he went, fires of revival broke out in towns and cities. He eventually spent more than ten years of his life tirelessly preaching in the Colonies. He began in Philadelphia, then journeyed to New York, south to Savannah, Williamsburg, Charleston, and many other cities, as well. Great multitudes flocked to hear him. No building was sufficiently large enough to accommodate the people. From pulpits to town squares and corn fields, he would preach – often to thousands at a time – his melodic voice and dramatic gestures providing him with great personal magnetism. People would gather from miles around to hear him present "a gospel that was sufficiently old to be easily understood and sufficiently new to provide the savor of novelty."[19]

The revival of 1740 was more than the result of one man's preaching. "Showers of refreshment" were being poured out from heaven. Whole towns and cities were being swept under the power of God's irresistible grace. "From being thoughtless and indifferent about religion, it seemed as if the world was growing religious; so that one could not walk through the town in an evening without hearing psalms sung in different families in every street."[20]

During 1741 and 1742, powerful revivals were experienced at Natick, Wrentham, Bridgewater, Taunton, Maldleborough, Halifax, Gloucester, and Reading in Massachusetts. Multitudes of other places were visited with revivals varying power. In some places the revivals were ignited through the preaching of Whitefield and Tennant, but elsewhere, awakenings sprang forth through the efforts of visiting ministers or evangelists.[21]

These revivals were often accompanied by unusual behavior on the part of the hearers. Rev. Jonathan Parsons, a pastor at that time, describes the unusual power visible upon the people. "Many had their countenance changed; their thoughts seemed to trouble them, so that their loins were loosed, and their knees smote one against another. Great numbers cried out in anguish of soul." Stout men fell as though they had been shot through the heart. Some young women were thrown into hysteric fits. Often those preaching would stop and ask the people to regain their composure before they could proceed.[22]

By the close of 1742, all of New England was ablaze with the fervor of revival. Scarcely a parish existed that did not experience some measure of fruit from the Great Awakening. The outpouring of the Spirit swept through the south as well, in spite of opposition from the established church. Much of the work in the south was carried out by laymen, urged on by the spiritual hunger of men and women wanting more of God.

The Great Awakening in America, so aptly described, was the result of various revivals throughout the land. As already mentioned, numerous men were used mightily by God through the gift of preaching. If any one man, however, stands out as a key individual of the Revival, it would probably be George Whitefield. Yet, when all was said and done, little or no dependency upon external measures was the means for promoting this work of grace. God, in His sovereignty, had indeed accomplished His purposes independently of man's agency or cooperation. Prayer, however, did play an important role in the revival. The records of the Great Awakening clearly depict the leaders of that day as men of prayer.

In fact, if any one factor could be seen as contributory to the 1740 Revival, it was the effective, fervent prayers of the righteous.

THE GREAT AWAKENING IN ENGLAND
(THE WESLEYAN REVIVAL)

After fifty years of religious skepticism and moral depravity, England experienced one of the greatest revivals of all times. It began in 1739 and made steady progress until the end of the Eighteenth Century. Every revival of history has produced some degree of change within society, and this revival must be ranked among the top. An indelible mark was made upon the consciousness of the English people. Lives were radically changed.

Historians often attribute the 1739 revival to the influence of a few individuals endowed with a genius for leadership and organization. These men were also noted for their zealous spirit, eloquent preaching and relentless measure of energy. Indeed, like the Great Awakening in America, key individuals also played a vital part in the English revival. Yet, in the final analysis, the hand of God was behind it all.

Toward 1730, several Oxford students, formed a small religious society called the "holy club." They prayed together and ministered to the sick and those in prison. While their piety astonished and shocked the city, their efforts were quickly met with criticism and ridicule. Soon they became known as the "Club of Saints" or the "Methodists."[23] Three of these men were significant contributors to the revival. They were George Whitefield and Charles and John Wesley.

Having completed their studies, they dispersed to the mission fields of England and America. After years of little success, they were reunited toward the end of 1738. Although these men were extremely zealous and highly disciplined in their religious service, they lacked the power of God to convert others. Their lack of assurance of God's peace, along with their apparent failures in ministry, eventually led them to a true conversion experience. Whitefield, through a serious plight of illness, encountered the grace of God in the spring of 1735. He later testified that "God was pleased to remove the heavy load, to enable me to lay hold of His dear Son by a living faith and by giving me the Spirit of adoption, to seal me even to the day of everlasting redemption."[24] John and Charles Wesley were challenged by the faith they saw in the Moravians. Upon inquiring about this faith, Peter Boehler, a Moravian pastor, gave them the key: "Preach faith until you receive it." A short time thereafter, May 21, 1738, Charles Wesley was converted, while seeking God on his own. John was gloriously transformed three days later on May 24, 1738, at the well-known Aldersgate Society meeting. He testified of a deep and unmistakable experience of faith. His "heart was strangely warmed."[25]

Reunited in London (not at Oxford) in 1738, they began to preach on justification by faith and crowds flocked to hear them. Their fiery, eloquent sermons met with great success among the people. However, Church authorities soon became envious and shut their doors. Not to be denied the opportunity to preach, they turned to the streets and open fields. The revival of 1739 had begun. Immense crowds gathered about the Methodist preachers – one thousand, ten thousand, fifty thousand – up to eighty thousand gathered at a time. Their sermons were aimed at generating violent emotions, causing their listeners to despair over the dread of sin. They inspired fits of fainting and convulsions, only to eventually bring their audience to a mood of blissful peace.[26] Thousands were converted by their sermons.

They had hoped the Methodist "society" could remain a part of the Anglican Church, a kind of third order, working with the clergy to revitalize the Church. That however was not to be the case. Instead, they faced great opposition. The Church vehemently objected to their unorthodox style of preaching and their unconventional way of gathering an audience. Their sermons were more emotional than intellectual, and they were "offering Christ," inviting great numbers to make a decision involving the heart and mind.[27] This was unheard of in that day.

Hostilities increased in the early years of the 1740's. A widespread rumor was circulated that John Wesley was a papist in disguise. In the minds of many, he became a secret enemy to the country's liberty. The upper class Anglicans resented being told that their hearts were as sinful as a common wretch. On numerous occasions, rioting broke out and the Wesley brothers barely escaped with their lives. Yet, in many ways the persecution proved to be profitable. This revival was gaining nationwide publicity and a clear line of distinction was being drawn.[28]

Contrary to the fact that the Church of England stood in opposition to the revival, it proved to be to her advantage in the end. Prior to the 1740 awakening, the Anglican Church was dying of old age. The revival provoked her to jealousy. Eventually, much of the clergy adopted the

Wesley/Whitefield oratorical methods and fundamental doctrines. Nevertheless, their overall rejection of the revivalist, paved the way for the founding of a new sect. The Methodist Church would become the most powerfully organized, richest and largest of all Protestant denominations.[29]

Again we see how God graciously anointed the preaching – and praying – of several young radicals to give birth to a mighty move of His Spirit. The Wesley brothers and Whitefield were certainly not the only men who played a vital role in the revival, but these men did, indeed, lead the way. It is important, also, to note that much prayer preceded the birth of this revival. Upon the reuniting of the "Holy Club" in London in 1738, seven true ministers of Jesus Christ were joined together in nights of prayer and fasting.[30] These, of course, were not the only ones who had not bowed their knee to Baal.

Elie Halevy, writing in <u>The Birth of Methodism in England</u>, brings an interesting thought to mind. Wesley and Whitefield had sought to reawaken or revive the old Puritan faith which had triumphed a century before. In spite of the English liberalism and the religious despondency prevalent in the late Seventeenth Century, the seeds of the Puritan faith had been deeply planted in the roots of that nation. The formation of numerous religious societies around the turn of the Eighteenth Century, underscores the fact that many were hungry for the restoration of true spiritual faith.[31] Wesley and Whitefield were called to water the seed and the harvest was indeed plentiful. (1 Corinthians 3:6)

For almost fifty years, the Wesleyan revival swept across Britain, Wales, and Scotland. The powerful preaching of Wesley and Whitefield was multiplied many times over through lay preaching, which became an outstanding feature of Methodism. By 1790, the "societies," small organized groups of believers, boasted of over seventy-one thousand British members.[32] No movement of history was ever better supervised and organized than this move of God under the leadership of John Wesley. No other movement has produced greater social reform than has the Wesleyan Revival.[33]

EFFECTS OF THE GREAT AWAKENING IN ENGLAND

The Wesleyan Revival addressed more effectively the social problems of the Eighteenth Century than any other force. Its main effect was in the character change of the lower and middle class populace. Oppression of the poor had produced a hopelessness and complacency among the people. However, by 1755, thousands confessed to a newly acquired self -respect that made many repel the very suggestion of public aid.

Prior to the revival, the laboring poor were known for their lack of trust and irresponsibility for their own welfare. Severe working conditions and unregulated industrialism only served to make matters worse. Various attempts to deal with these problems proved futile. It was through Wesley's preaching that great numbers gained a sense of purpose and responsibility. His philosophy on the right use of wealth was based upon the foundation of Christian values, stressing the principle of stewardship. Masters must have a sense of responsibility for their workmen, likewise the workers must give honest labor to their masters. Idleness was regarded as a crime.[34] The following testimony of a humble Methodist supports the widespread philosophy of the revival.

> I determined that the business of my station should be done as well as it was in my power, and with all possible dispatch. I found by this method, I could do far more work in a day than I had done before, and have plenty of time for all the means of grace... Idleness and religion can never be reconciled together.[35]

Methodism did more for the relief of the poor, by encouraging them to support themselves, than all the legislative enactments in operation. Prudence and virtue became recognized as the strength and prosperity of the nation. Methodist preachers soon became welcomed in every city and Methodist workers were in high demand.

Another feature of the transforming effect of the revival was the abrupt disappearance of drunkenness. Methodism addressed this problem with violence. Anyone found inebriated was automatically expelled from the society. New converts found themselves occupying the chapel instead of the alehouse. Money that was formerly poured into the pockets of the alehouse keepers added increased earning power to sober workers and their families. Not only was the character of the nation being changed, but so also was the economics of the country undergoing change.[36]

The revived Methodist worked and lived austerely and found great satisfaction in doing so. Many combined their usual occupation with intensive work in the local society. They were committed to the propagation of the gospel. Many workers sought diligently to persuade their masters to become Methodist. This union of religious enthusiasm, Puritan austerity and a strong work ethic became marked characteristics of the revival.

Besides the social impact of the revival, political and educational systems were also affected. Wesley spoke out boldly against bribery and corruption in politics. He publicly condemned every form of political corruption and exhorted his followers to become involved in the voting process. He challenged people with the thought that, "whole elections depend on your vote." The Methodists soon became known as "the most incorruptible voters" in the realm.[37]

Wesley also pioneered an attack against slavery. In 1774, he published his "Thoughts on Slavery" and publicly denounced slave trade. He was the first man of national prominence to argue for the abolition of slavery. During the 1780 Conference of the Methodist Church in America, he declared that every person holding slaves was acting contrary to the laws of God and man. Wesley's influence among the Methodists proved to be a vital contribution in the abolition of slave trade.

In the area of education, Wesley and his followers promoted the growth of schools in a century when provision for education was glaringly inadequate. He started day schools in Bristol, Newcastle, and London; and his school at Kingswood became one of the finest public schools in the kingdom. During the next century, the Methodist became the greatest force in popular education.[38]

The Wesleyan Revival produced the greatest change in society in the history of modern man. It came at a time when the overall conditions of England were rooted in deep darkness. Social and political reforms enacted by the government were ineffective. Even the law had become powerless to bring about the needed change. Yet God, in His infinite mercy, chose once again to be gracious to man and send forth His Spirit. Although men like Whitefield and Wesley made a significant contribution to the revival, it was the power at work in the hearts of men that produced lasting results.

EFFECTS OF THE GREAT AWAKENING IN AMERICA

Interestingly enough, the Great Awakening in America produced similar results as that of the Wesleyan Revival. Was it because of the influence of Wesley and Whitefield in both revivals? That certainly must be part of the explanation. Yet we must give glory to whom glory is due. Often times throughout history, when God burdens and/or directs His church in a specific way in one location, He may place the same emphasis upon others thousands of miles away. Indeed there are no limitations on the Spirit of God. It is also important to note that in times of revival, man's awareness to the conditions of life around him is heightened. We become much more aware of the need for change and thus changes are produced.

The Great Awakening brought about significant growth in the Church, both spiritually and numerically. Careful historians have estimated that from 25-50,000 new converts were added to the churches of New England. The population in New England in the 1750's was 340,000.[39] That means that between 7.3% and 14.6% of the population was converted and brought into the Church. If we were to compare those percentages to our current population of 250,000,000 in America, a modern day revival with equivalent results would touch 18,000,000 - 36,500,000 people. That's significant growth for a ten year period.

Another notable outgrowth of the revival was the founding of two new denominations, the Separates and the Separate Baptists. Prior to this time, little tolerance was allowed for any group outside of the Anglican or Congregational system. However, after the First Great Awakening, it was impossible to hold dissenting groups in check. By 1755, one hundred and twenty-five Separate churches and seventy Separate Baptist churches were established in New England.[40] The Anglican churches also experienced numerical increases as many of the conservative, upper class people were touched by the revival. Finding the enthusiasm of the awakening too disorderly and the new evangelical Calvinists too pious for their tastes, they sought the security of the more conservative Episcopal structure.

Spiritually speaking the Awakening brought a restoration of Biblical truth. As mentioned earlier in this section of the paper, the Biblical standards in the churches prior to the Awakening were watered down in an attempt to reach the masses. Instead it simply filled the churches with unconverted sinners. The revival brought forth a clear, scriptural statement of one key truth: The reality and necessity of the "New Birth." Preaching was centered on the cross, salvation by faith in Christ and the sovereignty and holiness of God.[41] Men were brought under the convicting power of the Holy Spirit and called to repentance. The churches were once again filled with genuine born again believers.

Another result of the Awakening was a renewed emphasis in missions and education. George Whitefield not only championed the cause of the black man against slavery, but Whitefield also had a burden for the evangelization of the blacks. At one point, Whitefield was actually indicted for holding religious meetings for Negroes. Eventually other pastors, supporters of the revival, joined the ranks by encouraging masters to instruct their Negroes in the Christian faith.[42] Later the Methodists and Baptists played a major part in evangelizing the blacks.

Around 1743, David Brainerd, a revival convert, began his extensive missionary labors among the Indians in Massachusetts. His labors were abruptly ended by his early death but his biography, written by Jonathan Edwards, became a classic of devotion and inspired many to follow in his footsteps. Henry Martyn, reading the accounts of Brainerd's life and devotion, was so moved that he became the first missionary to the Moslem world.[43]

Even more significant than the renewed interest in missions was the interest in education. Numerous colleges were the direct fruit of the revival. Among them are: Princeton of the Presbyterians; Dartmouth of the Congregationalists; Brown of the Baptist; Rutgers of the Reformed and the University of Pennsylvania can be traced back to George Whitefield as its original founder. Many of these schools were founded for the purpose of preparing men for ministry.

And finally, but not least among the products of the Awakening was its influence upon the political life and future of the nation. The expansion of the newer denominations paved the way for tolerance of opinion and liberty of conscience. This guaranteed religious liberty gave birth to a unifying influence throughout the nation. The Great Awakening touched all classes, colors, and creeds, helping to break down the barriers of intolerance and aloofness that existed prior to that time. Although the colonies were deeply involved in wars and political turmoil during the next forty years, the preserving influence of the revival enabled America to emerge from the struggle a Christian nation.

NOTES:

[1] Earnest H. Bacon, Heir of the Puritans, p. 103.
[2] Arnold Dallimore, George Whitefield (Vol. 1), p. 19.
[3] Ibid., p. 23.
[4] Henry Fielding, An Enquiry into the Late Increase of Robbers, p. 19.
[5] Albert D. Belden, George Whitefield - the Awakener, p. 53.
[6] J. Wesley Bready, England: Before and After Wesley, p. 127.
[7] Ibid.
[8] Ibid., p. 133.
[9] Arnold Dallimore, George Whitefield, p. 29.
[10] Michael McGiffert (ed.), Puritanism and the American Experience, pp. 94-95.
[11] Fred W. Hoffman, Revival Times in America, p. 43.
[12] Frank Greenville Beardsley, A History of American Revivals, p. 13.
[13] Fred W. Hoffman, Revival Times in America, p. 45.
[14] Frank Greenville Beardsley, A History of American Revivals, p. 15.
[15] Ola Elizabeth Winston, Jonathan Edwards, p. 202.
[16] Frank Greenville Beardsley, A History of American Revivals, p. 27.
[17] William G. McLoughlin, Revivals, Awakenings and Reforms, p. 45.
[18] Fred W. Hoffman, Revival Times in America, p. 50.
[19] Ola Elizabeth Winslow, Jonathan Edwards, p. 177.
[20] rank Greenville Beardsley, A History of American Revivals, p. 38.
[21] Ibid., p. 42.
[22] Ibid, p. 43.
[23] Elie Halevy, The Birth of Methodism in England, p. 36.
[24] Arnold A. Dallimore, George Whitefield, p. 77
[25] Wilson Engel (Editor), Christian History Magazine, p. 9.
[26] Elie Halevy, The Birth of Methodism in England, p. 37.
[27] Rupert Davies, (Ed), A History of the Methodist Church in Great Britain, p. 53.
[28] Ibid., p. 55.
[29] Elie Halevy, The Birth of Methodism in England, p. 37.
[30] Arnold A. Dallimore, George Whitefield, p. 222.
[31] Elie Halevy, The Birth of Methodism in England, p. 43 45.
[32] Kenneth Scott Latourette, A History of Christianity, (Vol. II), p. 1027.
[33] Charles P. Schmitt, Root Out of Dry Ground, p. 109.
[34] Rupert Davies and Gordon Rupp, (General Editors), A History of the Methodist Church in Great Britain, (Vol. 1), p. 60.
[35] Wellman J. Warner, The Wesleyan Movement in the Industrial Revolution, p. 169.
[36] Ibid., p. 171.
[37] Rupert Davies and Gordon Rupp, (General Editors), A History of the Methodist Church, p. 65.
[38] Ibid., p. 67.
[39] Frank Greenville Beardsley, A History of American Revivals, p. 64.
[40] William G. McLoughlin, Revivals, Awakenings and Reforms, p. 67.

[41] Fred W. Hoffman, <u>Revival Times in America</u>, p. 60.

[42] Charles Hartshorn Maxton, <u>The Great Awakening in the Middle Colonies</u>, p. 92.

[43] Fred W. Hoffman, <u>Revival Times in America</u>, p. 61.

THE GREAT REVIVAL
(SECOND GREAT AWAKENING)
1787-1805

CONDITIONS PRIOR TO THE GREAT REVIVAL

As Isaac Weld, a British traveler, made his way across Virginia in 1796, he noted widespread addiction to alcohol, contentment of living and – most of all – decayed and empty churches.[1] How could this be? Only sixty years earlier the nation was aflame with the fires of revival born from the First Great Awakening. Now, the fire was all but extinguished; only some smoldering ashes remained.

Such is the pattern of spiritual life in the history of man. "When all the generations had gathered to their fathers, another generation arose after them who did not know the Lord nor the work which He had done for Israel." (Judges 2:10) Religious bickering and jealous controversies during the latter years of the Great Awakening brought an abrupt end to the active work of the revival. As the effects of spiritual decline became evident, the mighty manifestation of the Spirit's power ceased. Gone from the hearts of many Christians was the spirit of prayer and earnest seeking for the will of God. By the late Eighteenth Century, coldness and formality ruled the Church once again.

However, not all the spiritual fervor of the Great Awakening was immediately lost. The fires of revival lingered in some places more so than in others, and a residue of life remained. For example, the preaching was more spiritual than it had been before the revival, the great doctrines of redemption more faithfully proclaimed. Also, the missionary efforts of the Church were more zealous after the revival. Though the years between the First Great Awakening and the Great Revival were comparatively dark, at no time during the spiritual dearth was it all darkness. There were local revivals in scattered places in every section of the Colonies. Interdenominational revivals among the Baptist, Methodist, and Presbyterians helped to strengthen the force of religion from time to time.[2] A number of awakenings occurred in some of the colleges, notably at Princeton and Yale. Yet, there was no Great Revival movement, no manifestations of spiritual power such as in the days of 1740 and most churches sank slowly back into a condition of lethargy and discouragement.[3]

The spiritual decline of the late Eighteenth Century can be attributed to a number of different factors. One major issue had to be the disturbed political and social conditions of the day. Shortly after the main thrust of the Great Awakening, the Colonies were plunged into the bloody French and Indian War (1754-1763) and then the Revolutionary War (1775-1783). All at once, the frontiers were in constant danger of attack and massacre, and hostilities were increasing between the Colonies and England. Families and communities were often divided in their sympathies, and quarrels and bitterness ensued. Eventually, disputes over taxation and other forms of imposed government culminated in the Revolution. The war not only brought years of struggle and suffering, but also the usual undermining of morality associated with military conflict. For instance, drunkenness and licentiousness increased at an alarming rate. Everyone – including the clergy – seemed to focus their efforts on war, and religion was neglected.

John Fiske, the American historian, refers to the years following the Revolution as, "the critical period of American History."[4] The Colonies were impoverished and exhausted. The new states disagreed with one another and the central government they had erected. The new economy was struggling, and those living under the financial crunch resisted the imposition of taxes. As a result, a number of tax rebellions broke out, such as the Whiskey Rebellion in Pennsylvania and Shay's Rebellion in Massachusetts. These were quelled with armed force, and the nation toddled onward. Religion, however, in these years reached the lowest mark in all of our history.

In the political realm, confusion and division characterized the times. While there was general agreement on the nation's achievements and potential, there was considerable disagreement on how to proceed. After the passing of President George Washington, two political parties emerged, one led by Thomas Jefferson and the other by Alexander Hamilton. Jefferson appealed to the simple farmers of the rural South and West, arguing on behalf of an alliance with France. After all, it was the French who helped subsidize the Colonies during the Revolutionary War.[5] Hamilton, on the other hand, proposed a program to develop a mercantile, commercial, and manufacturing nation. He envisioned cities with a strong army and navy to protect them from foreign interest. Hamilton's foreign policy was exactly the opposite of Jefferson's. It included an alliance with England against Napoleon.[6] As could be expected, these widely different programs promoted doubt and unrest within the young nation.

In addition to the general instability of the times, the Church was inundated with a flood of rationalistic literature from France and England. French officers and soldiers brought infidelity, skepticism, and the tenets of deism into the country during the Revolutionary years. America was ripe for revolutionary ideas, not only in politics and government, but in religion as well, and the rationalistic philosophy took root.

Thomas Paine wrote a book entitled <u>The Age of Reason</u>, which was an attack upon both atheism and Christianity. The book was published in France and sold in America for a few cents. Where it was banned, it was given away. The effect on U.S. colleges was disastrous with hundreds of students embracing rationalism. Bible colleges became centers of skepticism, and the anti-Christian teachings of deism were almost universally adopted. Dr. Timothy Dwight, then president of Yale College, described the flood of rationalism in America this way, "The dregs of infidelity vomited on us ... the whole mass of pollution emptied on this country."[7] Since Paine had been active as a leader in the movement for independence, his work found ready acceptance among many of the political and intellectual leaders of the country. In all walks of life, infidelity and atheism became the popular doctrine of the day.[8]

In the religious realm, two philosophical views became the source of controversy within many denominations. The world view of Calvinism stressed man's depravity and untrustworthiness, while rationalism stressed man's innate goodness, free will, and reasonableness. Calvinists believed that the fate of men and nations lay in the mysterious and arbitrary will of God. God might, at any moment become angry with the nation because of its materialism, speculation, and neglect of worship. The deist, on the other hand, taught that God is benevolent, that He governs by reason, and that His laws are regular and beneficent. According to deism, God's chief aim is to promote the happiness and well-being of mankind.[9] The latter seemed to be more in harmony with the American experience and the widely accepted belief that "God helps them who help themselves," a popular phrase from Benjamin Franklin's Poor Richard's Almanac – not the Bible.[10]

Unitarianism and Universalism, both offshoots of the infidel movement, developed and spread throughout New England and the middle states. As the influence of the Christian church waned, a flood of corruption swept over the land. Profanity, alcoholism, gambling, promiscuity, pride, and every form of excess was thriving, but the very foundation of the nation was in jeopardy. Once again, America found herself in need of another revival.

THE GREAT REVIVAL
(SECOND GREAT AWAKENING)

With every revival, there is always a remnant of believers who are unwilling to give up and throw in the towel. So it was in this case, as well. In spite of the deplorable moral condition of the nation and spiritual apostasy in the church, a few godly men and women who believed had hope. They knew that God could save America and began to pray. In New England, a group of twenty-three ministers sent forth a circular letter calling for Christians to pray. In response, prayer groups sprung up all over New England. Individual congregations set aside days for prayer and fasting. As early as 1778, the North Carolina Kehukee Baptist Association called for a time of prayer and fasting to storm the throne of grace for revival. Again, in 1785, another fast was proclaimed, and the hunger for revival soon spread.[11] Local churches, neighborhood fellowships, and gatherings everywhere prayed for revival to come. As they sought the Lord with their whole hearts, He heard their cry and sent revival.

As early as 1787, there were powerful moves of the Spirit of God in parts of Virginia and Georgia. One such occurrence took place in Virginia at Hampton Sydney College, in which more than half of the student body was powerfully converted to Christ.[12] The revival soon spread to surrounding counties and many churches in the Virginia Valley experienced an unusual visitation of God's presence. The revival, however, did not touch New England until 1792, when an awakening of far-reaching influence took place at Lee, Massachusetts under the ministry of Alvin Hyde.[13] Here is Dr. Hyde's account of what took place during the early days of revival:

The first season of refreshing from the presence of the Lord which this people enjoyed commenced in June 1792, a few days after the event of my ordination. There was at this time no religious excitement in this region of the country, nor had I knowledge of there being a special work of God's grace in any part of the land. The church here was small and feeble, having only twenty-one male members. It was, however, a praying band, and they were often together, like the primitive Christians, continuing with one accord in prayer. Immediately upon being stationed here as a watchman, I instituted a weekly religious meeting to be held on each Wednesday, and in succession at the various schoolhouses in the town. These were well attended in every district, and enabled me to instruct the people, and to present the truths of the gospel to old and young in the most plain and familiar manner.

With a view to form a still more particular acquaintance with the people, I early began to make family visits in different sections of the town. These visits, of which I made a number in the course of a week, were used wholly in conversing on the great subject of religion, and in obtaining with as much correctness as I could, a knowledge of their spiritual state, that my instruction might be better adapted to their case. This people had been nine years without a pastor, and were unhappily divided in their religious opinions. As they had been in the habit of maintaining warm disputes with each other on the doctrines of the Bible, I calculated on having to encounter many trials. Contrary to my expectations, I found on my first visit, many persons of different ages under serious and very deep impression, each one supporting his own burdens and distress of mind on account of his sins, to be singular, not having the least knowledge that any others were awakened. It was evident that the Lord had come into the midst of us in the greatness of His power, producing here and there, and among the young and old, deep conviction of sin. A marvelous work was begun and it bore the decisive marks of being God's work. So great was the excitement, though not yet known abroad, that into whatsoever section of the town I now went, the people in that neighborhood would leave their worldly employments at any hour of the day, and soon fill a large room. Before I was aware, and without any previous appointment, I found myself on these occasions in the midst of a solemn and anxious assembly. Many were in tears and bowed down with the weight of their sins. and some began to rejoice in hope. These seasons were spent in prayer and exhortation, and in conversing with the anxious, and with such as had found relief in submitting themselves to God. This was done in the hearing of all who were present. Being then a youth of only twenty-four years, and inexperienced, I felt weak indeed, and was often ready to sink under this vast weight of responsibility, but the Lord carried me along from one interesting scene to another.

As yet there had been no public religious meeting except on the Sabbath. A weekly lecture at the meeting house was now appointed on Thursday, and though it was in the most busy season of the year, the house was filled. This lecture was continued for more than six months without any abatement of attention; in sustaining which I was aided by neighboring ministers, and by others who came to witness this display of divine grace. The work spread to every part of town, and was especially powerful among those who had taken their stand in opposition to the small church, and the distinguishing doctrines of grace. Many of this class were compelled, notwithstanding their former hatred of the truths of the gospel, to cry `What must we do to be saved?'

The truths which I exhibited in my public discourses were in substance the following: The holiness and immutability of God; the purity and perfection of His law; the entire depravity of the heart, consisting in voluntary opposition to God and holiness; the fullness and sufficiency of the atonement made by Christ; the freeness of the offer of pardon, made to all on condition of repentance; the necessity of a change of heart by the Holy Spirit, arising from the deep-rooted depravity of man; the utter inexcusableness of sinners in rejecting the overtures of mercy; and the duty and reasonableness of immediate submission to God. These are some of the truths which God appeared to own and bless, through the agency of the Spirit.

All of our religious meetings were very much thronged, and yet were never noisy or irregular, nor continued to a late hour. They were characterized by a stillness and solemnity which I believe I have rarely witnessed. The converts appeared to renounce all dependence on their own doings, feeling themselves entirely destitute of righteousness, and that all their hope of salvation was in the mercy of God in Christ. To the praise of the sovereign grace of God, I may say that the work continued with great regularity and little abatement, nearly eighteen months. In this time, as appears from the records of the church, one hundred and ten persons of different ages united themselves unto the Lord and His covenant people. All appeared to exhibit the fruits of the Spirit, and to exemplify the religion of Jesus in their subsequent lives. This revival of religion produced a surprising change in the religious sentiments and feelings of the people, and in the general aspect of the town.[14]

The revival in Lee, Massachusetts soon spread throughout the New England area. The Spirit of God awakened churches and entire communities. The pattern, initiated and sustained by prayer, was similar in many places.

Unlike the 1740 revival led by such men as Wesley, Edwards, Tennant, and Whitefield, this movement boasted no outstanding leaders. There were no fiery evangelists going about stirring the churches to repentance. Faithful, earnest pastors, laboring in their own communities did most of the work. God indeed was moving in a sovereign, powerful way, and all who would open their hearts experienced the breath of His Spirit.

Numerous college campuses were greatly affected during this time. Perhaps, it was because the light of the gospel shone brightly in the darkness caused by the infidelity and skepticism that had recently flooded American education. God does promise that "when the enemy comes in like a flood, the Spirit of God will lift up a standard against him," (Isaiah 59:19b) and that "where sin abound[s] grace abound[s] much more." (Romans 5:20) Hungry hearts on the campuses of America attest to these principles in God's Word.

For example, at Yale College, President Timothy Dwight took on the forces of infidelity and skepticism almost single-handedly. Dwight was the grandson of Jonathan Edwards, reared in a home of prayer and piety and nurtured in an atmosphere of revival. When he came to Yale, the school was already deeply affected by the philosophy of rationalism. Shortly after his arrival, he presented a series of sermons aimed at answering its arguments. In a masterful way, he attacked and overthrew the entire philosophy of the skeptics. He so completely revealed to the students their ignorance of the truths of scripture and so thoroughly destroyed their arguments that they never dared challenge him again. A remarkable change soon swept over the life of that campus and in 1802, seventy-five students out of an enrollment of two hundred and thirty were powerfully converted and added to the church. Nearly half of these converts later entered the gospel ministry.[15]

Frank Greenville Beardsley wrote in his book, A History of American Revivals, "the importance of such a factor in the religious life of the nation cannot be overestimated." Not only were men and women forever changed in the wake of this revival, but many went on to influence the lives of hundreds and possibly thousands of others. The events that took place at Yale College turned the tide away from the philosophy of deism and toward Christianity.[16]

A marked characteristic of this revival was the permanency it produced. During the years of 1792 to 1797, over one hundred and fifty churches in the New England area were visited with renewed spiritual awakening. The waves of revival extended throughout western Pennsylvania and northeastern Ohio. Between 1798-1800, the western portion of New York State was ignited, along with parts of Delaware. These revivals continued unabated for several years.

Yet, it was along the frontiers in the West and the South, that the awakening reached its most powerful climax and influence – and became known as The Second Great Awakening. In the Carolinas a young Presbyterian minister by the name of James McGready, lit a spark everywhere he preached. However, the excitement of his ministry in South Carolina was met with fierce opposition and, on several occasions, his life threatened for preaching the gospel. Eventually, he was forced to resettle in the southern part of Kentucky. There, he was committed to seeing revival come to Logan County and the rest of the world. He drew up a solemn covenant calling for special prayer every Saturday night, Sunday morning, and the third Saturday of every month. Within a year, signs of the Great Revival swept over the western and southern states.[17]

It was in Logan County, Kentucky that the first open air camp meetings were held. There, on the edge of the prairie, multitudes came together from a radius of up to sixty miles. The meetings would last several days and nights, accompanied by unusual phenomena. Men, women, and children would fall down – like men slain in battle – and remain in a breathless, in a motionless state for hours. Upon awakening, they would declare the wonderful works of God and the glorious mysteries of the gospel. It was obvious that the hand of God was bringing men to repentance, followed by times of fervent praise and thanksgiving.[18]

From Logan County, the revival spread to Bourbon County through the leadership of Barton Stone. Stone had visited Logan County and returned home with a desire to see God move in a similar way in Bourbon County. Stone made preparations to host a camp meeting at Cane Ridge in August, 1801. After months of planning the famous Cane Ridge Camp Meeting began on Friday, August 8, 1801. By Saturday, twenty to thirty thousand were assembled.

As the worshippers scattered across the hillside, four and five preachers spoke at the same time in different parts of the camp. Using every technique known to their profession, the ministers urged their listeners to consider the terrors of hell and imagine the glories of heaven. Multitudes were converted to Christ during the seven days that followed. Numerous miracles occurred, adding convincing proof of the presence of Almighty God. Even the skeptics could not deny the authenticity of the work of God.[19]

The Cane Ridge Revival gave birth to six distinct and unusual manifestations of revivalism. They became commonly known as the falling exercise, the rolling exercise, the "jerks," the barking exercise, the dancing exercise, and the laughing and singing exercises. These symptoms were received as uncontrollable responses to the manifestation of the Holy Spirit. John Boles in his book, The Great Revival, states that these revival exercises were probably restricted to a comparative few.

 Except at the very start, they were never a significant factor in the camp meetings. During most camp meetings, shouting, crying, and falling down were the only physical responses to passionate preaching![20]

Others argued that this "strange phenomena" was common among the frontier revivals. One thing that was clearly agreed upon, however, was the genuineness of the revival.

Entire communities were transformed by the camp meetings. Sobriety and morality replaced drunkenness and immorality. Visitors to Kentucky were quoted as saying, "Kentucky appears to be the most moral place I have ever seen."[21] Frank Beardsley, in his study of revivals, described the revival in Kentucky as "the most extraordinary that has ever visited the church of Christ."[22]

The Great Revival didn't end in Cane Ridge, Kentucky, but swept the entire South with amazing speed, touching portions of Ohio, western Pennsylvania, and Maryland. Before it would end, the movement would affect the entire nation. In the South, every denomination experienced the power of this sovereign work of God. In particular, the Presbyterians, Methodists, and Baptists were united in the revival, as they labored together on behalf of the souls of men. Crowds of over ten thousand were frequent at camp meetings in Tennessee and Kentucky. During the year of 1802, the Methodists boasted of adding three thousand new members in western Tennessee alone.[23] By 1803, the revival had spread back into western Georgia, North and South Carolina, Virginia, and as far north as parts of Canada.[24]

The main thrust of the Great Revival lasted about five to six years. By 1805, the reports had all but diminished. Although, as late as 1809, interdenominational camp meetings were still being held in the South. As with every revival, this one had a beginning and an end. Once again, the hand of God was being lifted from the nation, and a time of testing would prove or disprove the authenticity of the awakening.

Approximately a decade later, however, a man of unusual anointing and boldness emerged upon the scene. Charles Finney, whom many consider to be the "Father of Revival," was, perhaps, the most impressive religious revolutionary that America has ever produced.[25] Everywhere he went, revival followed, and for forty years, Finney was used mightily by God to prick the heart of the nation. It is documented that over half a million people were converted through his ministry. Finney repudiated the teachings of Calvinism, which emphasized the sovereignty of God with regard to election in the salvation of man. Instead, he preached that man was given a free will, and that the salvation – freely given on Calvary – was a matter of personal choice.[26] Finney's messages were aimed at persuading his listeners to give themselves to God and change the way they were living in exchange of a life of holiness. He was not only effective in rekindling the fires of the Great Revival, but also revolutionized the Church's understanding of salvation, itself. Charles Finney served as a link between the Great Revival and the Prayer Meeting Revival of 1857.

EFFECTS OF THE REVIVAL

The Great Revival/Second Great Awakening produced an amazing turn-about in the philosophical and moral attitudes of the nation. As mentioned earlier, the rationalism and deism that flooded the country during the Revolutionary War overwhelmed America. By the latter part of the Eighteenth Century, this spirit of unbelief affected every walk of life. Colleges and universities rejected the teachings of Christianity with open contempt. Churches experienced a dramatic decline in membership, and the foundational beliefs of our forefathers were all but entirely rejected. It was at this hour that the revival touched the heart of our country.

The forces of infidelity were overthrown and defeated in the wake of the revival. Skepticism lost its influence, and the nation became Christian in character for many years to come.[27] The critical battleground of education was, for the most part, restored to the influence of Christian beliefs. Yale, Dartmouth, Williams, and various other institutions of higher learning became centers of Christian influence.[28]

Some historians also believe that the Revival of 1800 saved the nation from moral disaster. War had left the country in a state of spiritual apathy, the absence of religion meaning the absence of absolutes in the standards of society. When men are left to themselves, unrighteousness will tend to rule the land. Indeed, this was the case in the years before the Great Revival, but "where sin abound[s], grace abound[s] much more." (Romans 5:20)

Such was the case with this revival, as righteousness overtook the forces of degradation. Writing almost thirty years after the revival, Rev. Dr. Cleland, commented on its fruit.

> The work at first was no doubt a glorious work of God. Many within my knowledge became hopefully pious, the most of whom continue unto this present. The number of apostates was much fewer than I supposed.[29]

Others writing around that time reported that entire communities were transformed in the aftermath of the Great Revival. Drunkards, profane swearers, liars, and quarrelsome persons were remarkably transformed. The minutes of the General Assembly of the Presbyterian Church in 1803 stated that a profound change had taken place in society.

Drunkenness and disorder were being changed to sobriety, order and purity. By and large, moral disorder and vices no longer captured the attention of the people. Most individuals were devoting their time and thought to the things that make for righteousness.[30]

Almost all churches experienced abnormal growth during the revival. For example, in Kentucky alone the Baptist and Methodist Churches added over ten thousand members between 1800 and 1803. The Presbyterians, among whom the movement originated, reported an unusual increase in their membership as the result of the thousands being converted to Christ. It was impossible to determine with any degree of accuracy the number of actual converts during that time, but significant growth was reported in many denominations, as well as the organization of many new churches.[31]

More remarkable than the numerical growth, however, was the renewed spiritual life throughout the country. The last remnants of the ill-advised Half-Way Covenant were swept away. Churches that were receiving state aid broke their dependence and became self-supporting. Three new institutions were introduced into the life of the American church during this period: The midweek prayer meeting, the camp meeting, and the Sunday School. The midweek prayer meeting and the camp meeting started as a means of carrying on the revival, but continued as vital features in the life and ministry of the Church. The third institution, the Sunday School, had developed earlier in England and was now being imported into the American Churches as a great blessing.[32]

Once again, a renewed interest in missions was stimulated throughout the revival. As early as 1798, the Connecticut Missionary Society was formed for the purpose of reaching the heathen in North America and promoting Christian knowledge in new settlements throughout the country. That same year the Northern Missionary Society in the state of New York was formed. In 1814, the New England Tract Society was formed, which changed its name to the American Tract Society in 1823.[33] In all, over thirteen missionary societies were formed during the years of the revival and immediately thereafter. The Moravians also continued their work among the Indians, assisted by the Baptists and Presbyterians, and the Methodist "circuit riders" continued to migrate West, as the frontiers expanded. Also in 1816, the American Bible Society was established in an effort to supply new settlements with Bibles. Foreign missions were also improved through the work of the American Board of

Commissioners, formed in 1810.[34] All in all, missionary endeavors greatly accelerated as a result of the Great Revival.

Another issue that the revival influenced was slavery. Earlier movements for emancipation among the Baptists, Methodists, and Presbyterians intensified in the spirit of the visitation. In 1805, the Baptists in Kentucky excluded from fellowship a number of prominent slave holders. Barton W. Stone made the statement that "this revival cut the bonds of many poor slaves, and this argument speaks volumes in favor of the work."[35] Bit by bit, movement after movement, light was sinking into the hearts of men dispelling the darkness.

However, not all of the events of the revival were totally positive. It was noted in the journals of several camp leaders that immoral practices were frequent – even during camp meetings. One preacher stated that acts of immorality took place on the grounds under cover of darkness. Regarding his own congregation he wrote, "Some of the women who were the most persistent victims of the falling exercise were the ones prone to forget the edict of virtue. Several 'got careless' and are now pregnant with child." To prevent "carelessness" the leaders instituted "Night Watches" at camp meetings, beginning with the one at Sugar Ridge, Kentucky during August of 1802. These "Night Watches," as they were called, consisted of two men patrolling the grounds and meeting houses to deter immoral behavior.[36]

Another possibly negative by-product of the revival was a major division in the Presbyterian Church. The conflict began in Kentucky and Tennessee, when the pro-revivalists faced bitter opposition from the anti-revivalists. Those who had not personally experienced the revival were offended by the bodily exercises (such as falling, the jerks, barking, etc.) and were quick to make known their objections. Having little patience with the disorderly meetings of the revival, they strove to maintain the established form of worship.

In the fall of 1803, the controversy escalated, when two revival preachers were charged with disseminating doctrines contrary to the Presbyterian Confession of Faith. One of these men, Richard McNemar, was then placed on trial for preaching anti-Calvinistic doctrines. Four other revival preachers united with him in protest of the actions of the Washington Synod. Eventually, the five were suspended from the Presbyterian Church and established a their own presbytery in Springfield. Known as the "New Light," these men continued to pursue the spiritual life that was born through the revival. In the end, the schism resulted in the total desolation of the Presbyterian Church in Kentucky and part of Tennessee.[37]

In spite of the objectionable features and the bitter controversies that accompanied the revival, the overwhelming effects were positive. Thousands of backsliders were renewed to spiritual activity, Church attendance multiplying even more dramatically than the membership increased.[38] Many were converted to Christ and became involved in ministry and missions.[39] Society as a whole was once again transformed by the power of God, and the Church of Jesus Christ marched ahead triumphantly.

NOTES:

[1] John B. Boles, <u>The Great Revival</u>, p. 14.

[2] Ibid., p. 8.

[3] Fred W. Hoffman, <u>Revival Times in America</u>, p. 64.

[4] Ibid.

[5] <u>The New Encyclopedia Britannica</u>, Vol. XXIX, pp. 217-219.

[6] William G. McLoughlin, <u>Revivals, Awakenings and Reforms</u>, p. 99.

[7] Winkey Pratney, <u>Revival</u>, p. 11.

[8] Fred W. Hoffman, <u>Revival Times in America</u>, p. 66.

[9] William G. McLoughlin, <u>Revivals, Awakenings and Reforms</u>, p. 100.

[10] John Bartlett, <u>Familiar Quotations</u>, p. 347 # 15.

[11] John B. Boles, <u>The Great Revival</u>, p. 34.

[12] Fred W. Hoffman, <u>Revival Times in America</u>, p. 68.

[13] Frank Greenville Beardsley, <u>A History of American Revivals</u>, p. 85.

[14] Fred W. Hoffman, <u>Revival Times in America</u>, pp. 70, 71.

[15] Ibid., p. 73.

[16] Frank G. Beardsley, <u>A History of American Revivals</u>, p. 89.

[17] Catherine C. Cleveland, <u>The Great Revival in the West</u>, p. 40.

[18] Frank Greenville Beardsley, <u>A History of American Revivals</u>, p. 93.

[19] John B. Boles, <u>The Great Revival</u>, p. 66.

[20] Ibid., p. 68.

[21] Frank Greenville Beardsley, <u>A History of American Revivals</u>, p. 96.

[22] Ibid., p. 96.

[23] John B. Boles, <u>The Great Revival</u>, p. 73.

[24] Charles A. Johnson, <u>The Frontier Camp Meeting</u>, p. 68.

[25] Winkie Pratney, <u>Revival</u>, p. 125.

[26] William G. McLoughlin, <u>Revivals, Awakenings and Reforms</u>, p. 125.

[27] Fred W. Hoffman, <u>Revival Times in America</u>, p. 78.

[28] Frank Greenville Beardsley, <u>A History of American Revivals</u>, p. 101.

[29] Catherine C. Cleveland, <u>The Great Revival in the West</u>, p. 132.

[30] Ibid., p. 134.

[31] Fred W. Hoffman, <u>Revival Times in America</u>, p. 79.

[32] Ibid., p. 79.

[33] Frank Greenville Beardsley, <u>A History of American Revivals</u>, p. 104.

[34] Catherine C. Cleveland, <u>The Great Revival in the West</u>, p. 153.

[35] Ibid., p. 157.

[36] Charles A. Johnson, <u>The Frontier Camp Meeting</u>, p. 54.

[37] Catherine C. Cleveland, <u>The Great Revival in the West</u>, pp. 134-147.

[38] John B. Boles, <u>The Great Revival</u>, p. 83.

[39] Fred W. Hoffman, <u>Revival Times in America</u>, p. 79.

THE PRAYER MEETING REVIVAL
1857

CONDITIONS PRIOR TO THE PRAYER MEETING REVIVAL

Between 1845 and 1855, religious life in America was once again in decline, due to many political, social and religious factors.[1] It seems obvious, as we study various periods of history, that society as a whole is greatly affected whenever any of these three areas experience a dramatic change. For example, in this period, the nation met with unprecedented expansion and material growth.[2] This apparent "blessing" from God tempted many to pursue riches, while they ignored religion. Hence, the increase in man's material well-being altered the state of his spiritual life. The new prosperity caused many to become indifferent toward God, opening wide the door to the influence of evil. Each of these circumstances set the stage for another religious awakening.

In the spiritual realm, the Church went through an emotional upheaval between 1840 and 1845. An apocalyptic preacher by the name of William Miller predicted the return and reign of Christ on April 23, 1843. As the time drew near, the excitement of the second coming swept across the country. Great meetings were held and extensive preparation made for the Lord's appearing. Ascension robes were constructed, multitudes neglected their work and many who were rich generously sold their goods and gave to the poor. However, the day arrived, and Christ failed to return.

At this time, the leaders of the movement concluded that the time of the advent was really March 22, 1844. Again, the followers made ready for the coming of Christ. Once again the specified day came, but the Son of Man did not. Other dates were set, but they too were met with equal disappointment, staggering the faith of many. As in the days prior to the Great Revival, skepticism once again flooded the nation, and the Church became the subject of ridicule and abuse.[3]

Economic growth was another factor that influenced the spiritual climate in America. Many of those who became disillusioned with the Church gave themselves to the pursuit of material wealth, which was easily acquired at the time. Gold had just been discovered in California and much new land was available to squatters, thanks to the conquests of the Mexican War. Thousands of pioneers were crossing the plains to settled the West.[4] The new settlements meant an increase in trade, as cities and states were founded in rapid succession. Great leaps in population also had an effect on the new prosperity.[5]

An incredible arc in population also colored the picture, primarily on the East Coast. For example, in 1845 Ireland experienced a major famine, and thousands immigrated to America, the land of opportunity. Many other Europeans also flooded the nation during this period of history. The population of America grew from five million in 1800 to twenty-three million in 1850, to thirty million in 1860.[6] This rapid increase gave rise to dramatic expansion and industrial growth. Railroad building accelerated incredibly, quadrupling the railroad mileage of the country within a few short years. Gigantic schemes were proposed for internal national improvements, and many became preoccupied with "get rich schemes." Speculation became the craze of the nation, causing the rich to become richer and the poor to become poorer. Greed became the motive of many hearts.

In numerous cities, deep-seated, political corruption developed. The New York Tribune stated that during this time men of character and influence withdrew from government and allowed the cities to be ruled by those seeking personal gain. Thousands of rum sellers joined forces with armies of hoodlums to take control of major cities.[7]

On the national level, the issue of slavery intensified and created further division throughout the land. The North and the South were rapidly becoming divided. With the publication of Uncle Tom's Cabin and major court battles over slavery, the issue stayed before the minds of the people.[8] Should the nation become slave or free? Should it be united or divided? Was it to disintegrate, or should it stand as one nation, indivisible and sovereign? These issues stirred men to their depths, producing tense and bitter feelings in every corner of the country.[9]

Another consideration that greatly influenced the thinking of America was the increase in writing. It was in this period that the golden age of American literature was born. Prescott, Bryant, Longfellow, Whittier, Hawthorne, and Emerson produced numerous volumes during these years. Harper's Magazine regularly published excerpts of Dickens and Thackeray. Americans became avid readers during this time. Needless to say, the increase in daily and weekly newspapers exerted a powerful influence over the thinking of the nation.[10] In a positive way, the media played a powerful role in spreading the revival, which will be discussed more in depth in the next section.

Indeed this was an age of contrast and conflict. The nation was divided over issues, such as slavery and abolition, idealism and materialism, and humanitarianism and greed. Evangelical religion stood in stark opposition to the popular gospel of success.

Once again, America was in need of an invasion from the unseen world. Only God could open the eyes of the blind and readjust the course of the nation. Only God could break through the confusion and resolve the issues producing division. Only God could save America. Would He?

THE PRAYER MEETING REVIVAL

On October 14, 1857, America was shaken by a major financial crash. Greedy speculation, excessive railroad development, and a wild-cat currency system combined to bring about unexpected financial collapse. Hundreds of banks failed, railroads went bankrupt, and thousands of merchants were forced to close their doors. Factories were shut down and vast numbers of workers were thrown into unemployment. In New York City, thirty thousand men lost their jobs![11]

Overnight, the foundation of the country was shaken. Men looked into each other's faces and wondered, "What's next?" Every class was affected. Public confidence eroded. Multitudes became destitute and thousands walked the streets in idleness and hunger.[12] Stripped of their self-dependence, desperate men once again began to think about their need for God.

However, hard times do not always produce spiritual renewal. In 1827 there was a financial panic as widespread and disastrous as the one in 1857, yet life went on with little change regarding man's relationship with God. Later, in 1929, the most severe and prolonged business depression in the history of America seemed to produce no religious awakening whatsoever![13] Often men seem far more interested in examining the political and social causes for events than they are in evaluating their spiritual need. Although times of depression almost always precede a revival, they do not guarantee one. It is the sovereign intervention of God that causes men to turn back to Him.

Such was the case in the fall of 1857. It all began through the inspiration of a man by the name of Jeremiah Lanphier. He was employed as a lay missionary on behalf of the North Dutch Church in July 1857. In an effort to reach the unchurched, he was to call upon the families living in the vicinity of the church, distributing tracts and inviting people to the church and to the Lord.[14] As his efforts were met with great discouragement, Lanphier turned to prayer to find strength and courage. So blessed and encouraged was he through these times of prayer, that it occurred to him that others too might find help in their time of need through a prayer meeting. Therefore, he decided to begin a weekly prayer meeting at noon for the businessmen of New York City.

The first meeting was held on September 23, 1857 at the Fulton St. North Dutch Church. Although the meeting was widely publicized in homes, offices, and factories, the initial response was somewhat discouraging. For the first half hour, Lanphier prayed alone. Then, one by one, people came until a total of six were gathered for prayer. The following week, twenty attended and the week after that, forty. So encouraged were those in attendance that they decided to meet daily for one hour of corporate prayer. Week by week, the attendance increased, and by the end of four months, three rooms were crowded to overflowing. Soon the movement spread to other churches and other sections of the city. By the spring of 1858, more than twenty prayer meetings were held in New York City.[15]

Men of all classes attended the prayer meetings. Capitalists and laborers, manufacturers and artisans, professional men, merchants, clerks and men from various economic, social, and religious backgrounds came together to pray.[16] One of the unusual claims of this revival is that it bridged the barriers of denominationalism. Religion was put aside, as men humbly sought the help of God.[17]

Soon, the revival had spread to other cities and became headline news of the day.[18] Religious and secular newspapers all over the country began giving prominent notice to the noonday prayer gatherings. Eventually, reports of the revival took precedence over crime, politics, and even issues on slavery. For a period of time, revival news covered the front pages of many major newspapers. The New York dailies even published several extra editions, detailing the accounts and progress of the revival. Never before had religious news captured the interest of the secular media. Dr. J. Edwin Orr, in his book, The Fervent Prayer, states that there were two reasons for the media coverage. First of all the revival engrossed the whole nation. People were demanding revival news. Secondly, the revival had a startling effect on the editors and journalists themselves.[19] One thing was certain, the media played an important role in fanning revival fires.

By the summer of 1858, major prayer gatherings were occurring in numerous cities. In Chicago, the Metropolitan Theater was jammed daily with over two thousand in attendance.[20] In Philadelphia, not less than three thousand gathered at a single hall for the purpose of prayer.[21] James Hall, Handel Hall, Haydn Hall, and the American Mechanics Auditorium eventually overflowed into a great tent meeting in Philadelphia. Public high schools were used in Cleveland, Ohio for revival prayer meetings. Daily prayer had become so common that in one of Charles Finney's Boston meetings, a gentleman testified that he had traveled from Omaha, Nebraska to Boston and found daily prayer meetings in every city along the way.[22]

Not only were the large cities influenced by the revival, but thousands of smaller towns, villages and hamlets were transformed, as well. It was reported in New England that in some towns not a single person remained unconverted! The revival brought with it an uncanny conviction of God's Spirit, so that many were converted at work or while sitting alone in their parlor.[23] Every class of society was touched by this revival.

Colleges were once again greatly influenced. Nowhere were the awakened more effective and without fanaticism than in colleges and universities across the land. Oberlin College reported an awakening as early as November 1857 and became known as the citadel of evangelism. The New England colleges were stirred in 1858, when Dartmouth, Middlebury, Williams, and Amherst all reported powerful conversions of the student body. At Harvard, which was predominately Unitarian at this time, over two hundred students professed conversion and applied for membership at Yale's Congregational College Church. Of the two hundred and seventy-two students at Princeton, one hundred and two professed faith in Christ, and as many as fifty entered Christian service.[24] By 1859, hardly a single college or university was left untouched.

Although the revival was centrally located in the northeast section of the United States, it quickly spread across the entire nation and overseas, as well. Within a year or so, the United Kingdom, Ulster, Scotland, Wales, and England were moved by the revival. Ulster boasted of one hundred thousand converts, Wales claimed one hundred thousand, Scotland three hundred thousand, and England reported over half a million by 1865. Over a million converts were ultimately added to the churches of Great Britain![25] The revival also spread to other countries, such as India and southern Asia, through American missionaries. Eventually, it became known for its worldwide impact of reviving the spirit of prayer throughout the Church.[26]

Unlike most revivals that seem to center on the necessity of preaching, this revival focused on prayer. One remarkable account comes from the old battleship North Carolina, anchored in New York harbor. Over a thousand young men were stationed aboard the ship. Among these were four Christians who gathered to pray. As they prayed and worshipped the Lord, the convicting power of God swept through the ship causing many to cry out for mercy. Some of the most profane and ungodly men aboard were gripped with the conviction of their sin. Night after night, the prayer meeting was held and hundreds were converted, the ship becoming a mighty center of revival. Many converts were trained and sent to other naval ships, spreading the revival throughout the American Navy.[27]

A similar revival occurred among the Confederate Army in 1861. In the fall of that year, a revival of unusual power broke out among the troops stationed around Richmond, Virginia. It began in the hospital among the wounded and soon spread to the camps, as they returned for duty. The movement then spread to Tennessee and Arkansas. Encouraged by devout military leaders, such as Robert E. Lee and "Stonewall" Jackson, the revival moved throughout the entire

Confederate Army by 1863. By the end of the war, at least one hundred and fifty thousand soldiers were convicted and many more became praying men.[28]

EFFECTS OF THE PRAYER MEETING REVIVAL

Some historians have questioned whether the prayer meeting revival of 1857 should even be considered a major revival. Contemporaries of the time call it the "Businessman's Revival," as panic-stricken businessmen called for a noonday prayer meeting to avert disaster. These businessmen were sincere, but their prayers were essentially a ritual for God's assistance during a temporary business crisis.[29] Regardless of the cause or motivation, the results clearly speak of divine intervention in the affairs of human history.

Whatever was happening was quickly changing the nation. In New York alone, over two hundred towns reported having revivals at one time. In one year, over ten thousand converts were registered in the city of New York.[30] America, as a whole, experienced over one million conversions during a two-year period. During a period of six to eight weeks, when the revival was at its peak, it was estimated that fifty thousand persons were converted weekly.[31] Almost all denominations recorded an increase in membership during this time. In addition to the new converts, many believers were also revived and strengthened. Each class of society was affected – from the wealthy merchants to the lowly laborers, the social and ethical effect of this revival continuing for almost half a century.[32]

Every revival in history has been met with some degree of resistance. The Great Revival of 1800 met with fierce opposition from the conservatives who labeled the behavioral responses as fanatical. Many key revivalists, men such as Wesley, Whitefield, and Luther endured hostility and threats. However, the Prayer Meeting Revival faced very little opposition. As such, it may very well be considered the most widely accepted revival in history. Though it was of less force in the South than in the North (most likely due to the slavery issue[33]), it was publicly opposed by only one man, the Rev. Theodore Parker.

Mr. Parker was an American theologian of rationalist views, noted for his extreme opinions in theology. Upon attending a union prayer meeting in Boston, Mr. Parker offered a prayer. A zealous conservative, however, also stood and told the gathering that the man who just prayed was really outside the fold and needed prayer. He then proceeded to offer prayers for Theodore Parker's conversion. Greatly offended, Mr. Parker began to adamantly to oppose the revival.[34]

Why was the revival so widely accepted? Two notable observations that very well may have contributed to its overall acceptance are: (1) It was born through and carried out primarily by laymen, and (2) No one person seemed to dominate the leadership.

The traditional predominance of the clergy in regard to the ministry of the Church now gave way for the enthusiastic participation of lay leadership.[35] Laymen came to realize that they, too, have a part in the extension of Christ's kingdom. The newly awakened laity infused new energy and life into the ministry of the churches. The revival itself served as a training ground for lay leadership and brought to light the abilities of such men as D.L. Moody, who in turn became one of the greatest evangelists in the history of American Christianity.[36]

Also, the central force of this revival was not the powerful or eloquent preaching of any one individual. Once the revival began, many noted preachers determined that they must preach to further the revival. However the prayer meetings conducted by laymen, were as well attended, if not even more so, than the preaching services. No key individual was the force behind this revival. The fervent prayer of humble men was the key to power in this revival.[37] Together, these two elements further pointed to the fact that this revival was indeed the work of God.

Numerous other spiritual advancements can be attributed to this revival. A "spirit of prayer" was reborn in the Church and throughout the nation as well. Faith in prayer was raised to a new level with volumes written about instances of God's answers. Men and women from every walk of life began to pray for the power of God to rule their lives. One businessman was quoted as saying, "Prayer never was so great a blessing to me as it is in this time. I should certainly either break down or turn rascal, except for it!"[38]

The revival had a profound impact on the unity of the Church. Prior to the revival the various denominations viewed one another with feelings of mutual suspicion and distrust. Division kept the Church weak and powerless as a change agent in society. Yet, after the revival, believers from various backgrounds put aside their doctrinal differences to save souls from death. In 1877, Charles L. Thompson wrote, "The union movements inaugurated in 1857 have continued to the present and have been continuously effective in the enlargement of the kingdom of Christ."[39] Saints from numerous backgrounds not only prayed together, but also labored together. The unity born of this awakening was certainly more spiritual than is was organic. Supported by evangelicals from every denomination (a miracle in itself), it bridged the theological gaps that often keep the Church divided.

Another fruit of the revival was the genuine concern for the young people of society. It was widely accepted that if the country was to be taken for Christ, the decisive battle must be fought in the nursery and in the Sunday School. Children's ministry became a major concern and gave birth to Sunday School conventions geared toward training workers.[40] As a result, a concerted effort was made on behalf of the churches in reaching the young people of America.

Across the ocean, the problems facing the youth were much more severe. For example, in England children between the ages of seven and thirteen were shipped to other cities and bound by apprenticeship until they were twenty-one. Often forced to work fifteen or more hours a day, these children were mentally and physically abused. In the city of London, thirty thousand homeless children wandered the streets, naked and impoverished. The Prayer Revival in England stirred the hearts of many Christians, compelling them to action. Bramwell Booth, Lord Shaftesbury, and Josephine Butler led the Church in great victories that produced social reform.[41] Actually, the social changes from the revival were even greater in the United Kingdom than in America. This may have been due to the fact that the social conditions in England were much worse than those in the States...

While it is difficult to evaluate the overall effects of a revival in society, changes such as those mentioned above seem rather obvious. Others, however, may not be as readily observable. How can one gage the preserving influence that a revival has had on society? How are we to know what would have happened, had the revival not occurred? We cannot. Albeit, through the example below, we may be able to see how the spiritual climate of the day can affect the reception of political ideologies. Considering the life and teachings of Karl Marx, one could conclude that the 1857 Prayer Meeting Revival may have prevented Europe from turning to Communism...

Karl Marx grew up in Germany during the Lower Rhineland Revival, the son of Jewish believers. Karl was baptized as an infant and reared in a Christian environment as a young man. As an adult he moved to London, but met with personal tragedy. Marx lost three of his children through malnutrition during those early years in London, blaming their deaths on Christianity's failure to change the system. Embittered, he set out to destroy Christianity and everything it stood for. Karl Marx was committed to turning the world upside down by persuasion, denying God and promoting atheism.[42] His philosophies, however, did not gain wide acceptance in his day. Why?

History tells us that Karl Marx was able to have a powerful influence on society, but not until the Russian Revolution in the Twentieth Century. Actually, until then, it was little more than a nuisance movement. Why was this man, with his highly influential Communist philosophy, not an influence the European nations in his day? Perhaps it was because of the influence of the 1857 Prayer Meeting Revival.

Society, as a whole, was turned toward God. Although Marx was disillusioned and bitter, his generation did experience the transforming power of Christianity. Though Marx was blind to the fact that government was unable to turn the tide of evil, many of his contemporaries were not. In fact, many who were not preoccupied with blaming God, experienced this first-hand. Christianity could change society by changing the hearts of men. Christian ideals even became popular among those not professing faith. Perhaps, due to the present move of the Spirit of God, Marx's doctrines largely fell on deaf ears.

The revival, also, gave birth to the work and ministry of men and women who took a direct stand against Marxism. Lord Shaftesbury originated more social change through Parliament than all the other Parliaments of British history combined. In fact, he extended more benefits to all classes of working people than Marx ever did. Shaftesbury, along with other radicals like Catherine Booth, contradicted Marxism daily. To this day, the ministry of William and Catherine Booth, the Salvation Army, is the only religion officially banned in the Soviet Union.[43]

Although it is impossible to say what might have happened in Europe if Marxism had gone unchecked, it can be argued that the spiritual climate at the time did hinder its growth. Perhaps the philosophy of Karl Marx would have never been unable to overthrow the English political system – with or without the help of the revival. Perhaps. On the other hand, maybe all of Europe would have fallen prey to Communism. This writer believes that the 1857 revival was a key in preserving democracy and the freedom of Europe.

NOTES:

[1] J. Edwin Orr, The Fervent Prayer, p. 1.
[2] Fred W. Hoffman, Revival Times in America, p. 106.
[3] Frank Greenville Beardsley, A History of American Revivals, pp. 214-215.
[4] Fred W. Hoffman, Revival Times in America, p. 107.
[5] J. Edwin Orr, The Fervent Prayer, p. 1.
[6] Fred O. Hoffman, Revival Times in America, p. 107.
[7] Ibid., p. 107.
[8] Frank Greenville Beardsley, A History of American Revivals, pp. 213-214.
[9] Fred W. Hoffman, Revival Times in America, p. 108.
[10] Ibid., p. 107.
[11] J. Edwin Orr, The Fervent Prayer, p. 1.
[12] Charles L. Thompson, Times of Refreshing, pp. 158-159.
[13] Fred W. Hoffman, Revival Times in America, p. 109.
[14] Charles L. Thompson, Times of Refreshing, p. 160.
[15] Fred W. Hoffman, Revival Times in America, p. 110.
[16] Frank Greenville Beardsley, A History of American Revivals, p. 221.
[17] Charles L. Thompson, Times of Refreshing, p. 170.
[18] Timothy L. Smith, Revivalism and Social Reform, p. 63
[19] J. Edwin Orr, The Fervent Prayer, p. 35.
[20] Timothy L. Smith, Revivalism and Social Reform, p. 64.
[21] Charles L. Thompson, Times of Refreshing, p. 165.
[22] Frank Greenville Beardsley, A History of American Revivals, p. 227.
[23] Fred W. Hoffman, Revival Times in America, p. 114.
[24] J. Edwin Orr, The Fervent Prayer, p. 11.
[25] Winkey Pratney, Revival, p. 145.
[26] T. Edwin Orr, The Fervent Prayer, p. 6.
[27] Fred W. Hoffman, Revival Times in America, p. 114.
[28] Ibid., p. 120.
[29] William G. McLoughlin, Revivals, Awakenings and Reforms, pp. 141-142.
[30] Charles L. Thompson, Times of Refreshing, p. 166.
[31] Frank Greenville Beardsley, A History of American Revivals, p. 236.
[32] Winkey Pratney, Revival, p. 145.
[33] Fred W. Hoffman, Revival Times in America, p. 119.
[34] J. Edwin Orr, The Fervent Prayer, p. 37.
[35] Timothy L. Smith, Revivalism and Social Reform, p. 80.
[36] Frank Greenville Beardsley, A History of American Revivals, p. 237.
[37] Ibid., p. 228.
[38] Charles L. Thompson, Times of Refreshing, p. 161.
[39] Ibid., p. 170.
[40] Ibid., p. 163.
[41] T. Edwin Orr, The Fervent Prayer, p. 179.
[42] Ibid., p. 182.
[43] Winkey Pratney, Revival, pp. 147-149.

THE WELSH REVIVAL
1904 - 1912

Another revival of sizable magnitude and world-wide acclaim was the Welsh Revival of 1904. Born through an uneducated coal miner in a small town in Wales, this revival exploded overnight and eventually touched over fifteen major nations. Few books, however, were written its events, making research somewhat limited. What information we do have (taken from newspaper reports and verbal accounts, retold by eyewitnesses) validates this movement as a genuine revival of God.

What is it that separates a revival from other valid religious movements of history? James Stewart, in his book, Invasion of Wales by the Spirit, states three characteristics of a true revival: They are not begun or sustained by men, do not need organization or promotion, and, thirdly, Jesus Christ is the center of attention.

A genuine revival does not depend on human personalities to initiate it or keep it going, inasmuch as it is a work of God in the purest sense, orchestrated by the Holy Spirit. There is, of course, a human side to revival, as God does use human agents to fulfill His purpose, but it is God who initiates and concludes the hour of revival. The work of the Holy Spirit cannot be ordered, controlled or purchased by man. In fact, Stewart reports that not a single dollar was spent in advertising the revivalists.[1] Finally, the main characteristic of a true revival is that Jesus Christ, Himself, is the center of the attraction. During revival people gather for one purpose – to meet with God. In light of these characteristics, we will consider the events of the Welsh Revival.

CONDITIONS PRIOR TO THE WELSH REVIVAL

Although there was not a good deal of information available on the conditions prior to this revival, it was, however, a documented fact that Church membership in Wales was declining in the last decade of the Nineteenth Century. All the denominations were suffering from the loss of power in the pulpits and the worldly spirit among the members. Evan Phillips, a Moderator of the Presbyterian Assembly, declared in June of 1900 that revival was the greatest need of the Church. Until it came, meeting all other needs would be in vain.[2] Apparently, many others echoed his feelings, as well. As many as forty thousand believers throughout the country of Wales were desperately waiting for a fresh move of the Spirit of God.[3] They would not be disappointed.

Earnest intercession and a true brokenness and humility before God precede every outpouring of the Spirit. Such was the case in this revival, as well. At the age of thirteen, Evan Roberts began to pray that revival would come to Wales. His greatest passion in life was his interest in revival. Years later, he wrote to a friend that he would stay up all night to read or talk about revivals – and, of course, pray for revival. He faithfully attended church every night of the week for fear that God would visit a meeting, and he would miss it. However, after thirteen years of intercession – *revival came*.[4]

THE WELSH REVIVAL

It is amazing to see how God answers specific prayers that are prayed in accordance with His will. It is also amazing when He uses us to fulfill those prayers. The Rev. Seth Joshua was one such man. In 1904, he was a denominational evangelist with the Welsh Presbyterian Church. Noticing prevailing emphasis on intellectual qualifications for church leadership, Joshua prayed that God would use the most unlikely candidate – a lad from the mine fields of Wales – to revive His work. Not only did God hear his cry, but allowed Seth Joshua to be the man who would confirm that call on Evan Robert's life.[5]

At the age of twelve, Evan Roberts began working in the coal mines and, twelve years later, became a blacksmith. Still dissatisfied with his life's direction, in 1903, he offered himself to the ministry, passed the denominational examination, and entered Newcastle Emlyn Academy to prepare. While at Newcastle Emlyn, he attended a meeting conducted by Seth Joshua. At the close of the meeting, Joshua led the congregation in intercession for Wales. As he cried out in Welsh, "Lord ... bend us," Roberts knelt crying in great agony, "Lord, bend me!" In that moment of time, he felt a new power invade his soul, and he became concerned about others.

I felt ablaze with a desire to go throughout the length and breadth of Wales to tell of the Savior; and had that been possible, I was willing to pay God for doing so.[6]

Shortly thereafter, Roberts had a vision of all of Wales being lifted up to heaven. He began to tell others to prepare for the greatest revival that Wales had ever known. Surely it was coming, so he began to pray and believe God for one hundred thousand souls.

On October 31, 1904, Roberts returned home to conduct a series of meetings with the young people of his home church. Though his family was disturbed by his experience, his pastor opened the doors of the church to his ministry. That evening, after the regular prayer meeting, Roberts conducted a youth meeting with seventeen in attendance. At first, the people were unresponsive to his directives, but soon they all complied. The young revivalist preached on these four points for revival:

1. You must put away all unconfessed sin.
2. You must put away any doubtful habits.
3. You must obey the Spirit promptly.
4. You must confess Christ publicly.

Nightly meetings were held, and within a week the church was filled to capacity. The meetings would begin at seven p.m. and last until two or three a.m.! No one seemed concerned about the time. By Nov. 11, the Moriah Church was overcrowded with over eight hundred people. Many were on their knees crying out in deep distress, agonizing over the condition of their souls, and finding Christ as their personal savior. Soon the meetings spread to other locations as men and women met in homes and chapels to pray and praise the Master.[7]

As the revival grew and spread to other locations, it was consistently marked by intense prayer and glorious praise.[8] Once the Spirit began to move, preaching was seldom performed. Months later, after the revival gained world-wide recognition, many famous Christian leaders came to take part in the it. Few, if any, however, were given the opportunity to share in the pulpit. The meetings were led by the Holy Spirit from beginning to end; with even the most skeptical acknowledging that to be the case.

Journalists came from everywhere to evaluate and report on the authenticity of the revival. One such reporter was William T. Snead, the famous London editor of the Pall Mall Gazette. Upon his return home, he was interviewed by the London Methodist Times. The following excerpt seems to convey the kind of atmosphere prevalent throughout the revival:

"Well, Mr. Snead, you've been to the revival. What do you think of it?"

"Sir, the question is not what I think of it, but what it thinks of me, of you, and all the rest of us. For it is a very real thing, this revival, a live thing which seems to have power and a grip which may get hold of a good many of us, who at present are mere spectators."

"Do you think it is to march on then?"

"A revival is something like a revolution. It is apt to be wonderfully catching."

Further into the conversation, Mr. Snead continued to elaborate upon his experience...

Dread is not the right word. Awe expresses my sentiment better. For you are in the presence of the unknown. ... You have read ghost stories and can imagine what you would feel if you were alone at midnight in the haunted chamber of some old castle and you heard the slow and stealthy step stealing along the corridor where the visitor from another world was said to walk. If you go to south Wales and catch the revival, you will feel pretty much like that. There is something there from the other world. You cannot say whence it came or whither it is going, but it moves and lives and reaches for you all the time. You see men and women go down in sobbing agony before your eyes as the invisible Hand clutches at their heart. And you shudder. It's pretty grim I tell you. If you are afraid of strong emotions, you'd better give the revival a wide berth.[9]

Thousands were saved through this revival. By the year 1905, the Welsh Revival had reached full steam, influencing all classes, all age groups, and every denomination. The power of God was in their midst. Local newspapers reported the number of converts, recording seventy thousand in two months, eighty-five thousand in five, and one hundred thousand in half a year.[10] These numbers were from Wales alone – not to mention its impact in other places!

Although Evan Roberts was the key figure, the outpouring of God's spirit was not limited by his absence. One of the outstanding features of the Welsh Revival was the sense of the Lord's presence everywhere, throughout the entire nation – altogether apart from the young revivalist. It was not the presence of Evan Roberts that was felt, but rather the presence of almighty God.[11] Hallelujah!

Roberts, himself, was very concerned about his role in the revival. Whenever he sensed that people were coming to see him or hear him speak, he would immediately withdraw from the meetings. He dreaded newspaper reporters and avoided publicity at all costs. Roberts believed that if people would make him the center of attraction, the Spirit would withdraw and the revival would end. He was also very concerned that all the glory would be given to God and not to man. Soon the people understood that it was not Evan Roberts, but the Lord Jesus who was the author of this awakening. The believers in Wales were intensely proud of the young prophet, but they did not idolize him. They knew he was not the secret or cause of the awakening, only one of the chosen vessels.[12]

Like the Prayer Meeting Revival of 1857, this revival was marked by intense prayer and directed in many places through lay ministry. A typical revival meeting consisted of prayer, praise, confession, repentance, and testimonies. The meetings would begin as soon as part of the congregation assembled. No human leader was necessary. It was the spontaneous response to the prompting of the Holy Spirit that gave direction and order to these meetings. Often the meetings would begin at seven p.m. and last until three a.m., adjourning only to vacate the building for the early morning prayer meeting crowds. In many places, work would cease during the height of the outpouring. Factories and shops would close for up to three days at a time, and no one seemed to care.[13]

Evan Roberts believed that the key to revival was prayer, humility and obedience. Revival came because thousands of believers, unknown to each other, were crying out day after day for the fire of God to fall. The presence of the Holy Spirit brought a new depth of humility to the Church. As the Christians began to humble themselves and get right with God, the Spirit broke through in converting power upon the unsaved. The Holy Spirit was recognized and honored as a divine Person. The Christians obeyed Him immediately and without reservation. In so doing, they received the holy anointing that swept them onward as the conquering army of God.

If the formula for revival is so simple, why has the Church not embraced these principles? We could have a revival any time we want one! Ah, but let us not forget the sovereign aspect of revival. Indeed, from the human perspective, prayer, humility, and obedience may be the keys, but the formula is not complete without the sovereign hand of God. This writer believes that the Church is unable to effectively pray for revival without the inspiration of the Holy Spirit. Consider the words spoken through His prophet Isaiah...

I have set watchmen on your walls, O Jerusalem, who shall never hold their peace day or night. You who make mention of the Lord, do not keep silent, and give Him no rest till He establishes and till He makes Jerusalem a praise in all the earth. (Isaiah 62:6-7)

Unless God inspires the watchmen, our formulas are in vain. It is God who moves men to pray. It is God who brings us to a place of recognizing our desperate need of Him. As the psalmist so aptly stated, "Unless the Lord builds the house, they labor in vain who build it." (Psalms 127:100)

EFFECTS OF THE WELSH REVIVAL IN WALES

The impact of this revival was of world-wide significance. Beginning in Wales, it changed the entire composure of the country. The sale of alcoholic beverages dropped drastically and many taverns and pubs went out of business. In the Welsh metropolitan areas, the police reported a 60% decrease in drunkenness. In Swansea County, the police announced that there had not been a single charge for drunkenness over the 1905 New Year's holiday weekend. This was an all-time record.[14]

Political meetings were postponed, as members of the House of Parliament were found in revival meetings. Theatrical companies made sure they did not come to Wales for fear of going bankrupt. In many places magistrates were given white gloves to signify that there were no arrests. Prisons became empty, and the overall moral tone of the nation was changed.[15]

Attitudes of the workers improved, as did relationships between employers and employees. Long-standing debts were paid, stolen goods returned and vice became a thing of the past. Prayer meetings were conducted in factories and coal mines. In fact, cursing and profanity were so diminished that a "donkey strike" was reported in the mines. As the men gave up the use of foul language, the pit ponies, used to drag coal trucks, did not understand their commands. Confused, they just stood there – not knowing what to do!

The revival had a profound effect on the universities and colleges in Wales, as well as the grade schools. On many campuses, revival broke out and classes were cancelled. Many college students were spiritually revived and set ablaze with a love for Jesus. Even grade school children were touched and began holding their own meetings in homes, barns, and empty pigsties! The children also became an active part in public meetings through prayer, song, and exhortation.

During the years that the revival remained strong, entire towns were affected. Many churches remained open 24 hours a day to provide a place for people to meet and pray. In one community, an entire population was transformed into a praying community.[16] People everywhere were touched with a hunger for God. Thousands of lives were forever changed by this revival.

EFFECTS OF THE WELSH REVIVAL IN AMERICA

Thanks to the media, word of the Welsh Revival soon spread to other locations. The first to feel the fires were the Welsh-speaking colonies in America. The awakening began there in December of 1904, when Rev. J.D. Roberts was moved with news of the revival in Wales. Within a month, one hundred and twenty-three new converts were added to the Church in Scranton, Pennsylvania. Town by town and city by city, the revival swept through the churches, reviving members and converting outsiders.[17]

Soon the revival caught fire with the Baptists in Pennsylvania, the Methodists in Philadelphia, and the Young People's Society of Christian Endeavor in New Jersey. In Atlanta, nearly a thousand businessmen united in intercession for an outpouring of the Holy Spirit. Stores, factories, and offices closed in the middle of the day for prayer. Even the Supreme Court of Georgia adjourned so the politicians and lawmakers could participate in the prayer meetings! In a short time, practically every Christian denomination in the country was alive with the fervor of revival. The movement, with its Welsh counterpart, was characterized by an intense sensation of the presence of God in the congregations.

By the spring of 1905, the Methodists in Philadelphia were claiming ten thousand converts. On the New Jersey coast, there was such a stirring in Atlantic City that not more than fifty unconverted people remained in a population of sixty thousand. Despite the lack of large evangelistic campaigns, the churches of America were moved with great power. Not since the Prayer Meeting Revival of 1857 had this country been shaken as it was in the days when the Welsh Revival splashed upon the shores.[18]

EFFECTS OF THE WELSH REVIVAL IN CANADA

Canada was powerfully affected by the revival, as well. Churches from coast to coast were reawakened as Christians met together to pray. God, indeed, heard their cry and touched the nation at every level. Colleges and universities experienced a visitation of the Spirit, as did the collieries of Nova Scotia. Across the prairie, church after church was stirred. Even on the faraway Skeena River, the Indians were awakened.

In 1906, when R.A. Torrey was ministering in Toronto, two teenaged boys journeyed to the big city, after hearing about the revival. While attending the meetings, Ernest Gilmore Smith of the United Church of Canada and J. Oswald Smith of the Peoples Church in Toronto were gloriously saved. Thousands of others were also brought to Christ as a result of the Welsh Revival in Canada.[19]

EFFECTS OF THE WELSH REVIVAL IN LATIN AMERICA

Latin America experienced the waves of this revival, as well. For seven years, there was an upsurge in Brazil, beginning in 1905. While not of the same magnitude as in Wales, it did, however, rally the believers to prayer and evangelism. Record numbers were reported saved and hundreds of couples were legally married and added to the Church.[20]

In particular, a phenomenal revival did occur in the midwinter of 1905 among the Welsh colonists in Argentina. It spread to the Baptists, the Brethren, and eventually made great strides through the Pentecostals in that country. A Southern Baptist missionary wrote:

We are having a real revival. A special prayer meeting was followed each day by those attending going to homes and market places. As many as 300 attended each of the evening services. Never in Argentina have I seen such a manifestation of God's Spirit.

In Mexico City, news of the Welsh Revival stirred the English-speaking residents to prayer. In 1907 the Methodist Church experienced an unusual move of the Spirit of God. Night after night, believers were moved to tears and the unsaved were gloriously transformed.[21] Many other countries in Latin America were reportedly affected by the overflow of the Welsh Revival.

Several other nations experienced the power and influence of this revival through missionary work. For example, a young man who was personally involved in the Welsh Revival among the colliers went on to the mission field of South Africa with his wife. Rees Howells carried the fire of the Holy Spirit to a distant land and was used of God to stir the Church to a new level in its commitment to God. Another young preacher was so revolutionized by the Welsh Revival that he went to a Scandinavian country where today there is at least one hundred churches flourishing as a direct outcome of his ministry.[22] These are but a few examples of how this great awakening touched many parts of the world.

On the negative side, very little criticism was reported about the revival. Generally speaking, it was welcomed by practically every true denomination in the Church. It left behind a renewed emphasis of spiritual truth that changed the life of that generation for years to come. One sad note however was the personal tragedy regarding Evan Roberts.

Roberts was known to be bold and forthright when addressing concerns in the Church. On one occasion, he was invited to speak in a Congregational Church in the town of Dowlais. When it came time for him to speak, he stood and delivered a scathing "word from the Lord" that someone "near him" was "blocking the way of revival." He went on to say that unless it was dealt with, he would leave; he "would not take part in mock worship where the Holy Spirit was grieved." He left shortly thereafter.[23]

Peter Price, the pastor, was apparently offended by Roberts' comments. A week or so later he wrote a letter publicly denouncing Roberts and his ministry. He argued that there were two revivals going on in Wales, the real and the sham. He affirmed that his church was experiencing a genuine revival with hundreds of conversions. He also identified the "sham revival as a mockery; a blasphemous travesty of the real thing," and the chief figure was Evan Roberts. Price accused Roberts of using the language of Deity, as if he thought of himself as the fourth person of the Godhead. He further urged him to withdraw from ministry and learn a little more of the meaning of Christianity.[24]

A storm of violent protest and controversy ensued. Supporters of Roberts accused Price of jealousy and the spread of unfounded truth. Price's friends attempted to defend Price from the abusive criticism from Roberts' supporters. Roberts himself remained silent. Although he was deeply hurt by the public criticism, he refused to defend himself, making his primary concern the reputation of the Holy Spirit.[25] In the midst of growing disunity and under the strain of physical and emotional demands, Evan Roberts suddenly withdrew from public ministry. Offered a retreat home by a dear friend, Jesse Penn-Lewis and her husband, Roberts accepted and never returned to the ministry.

The revival continued on without him. It spread internationally, reviving the Church and bringing thousands to repentance. Roberts completely dropped out of ministry. He rejected all callers, ignored all letters, and refused to see even his own family members. Later he co-authored a book with Jesse Penn-Lewis entitled, War on the Saints. He spent the rest of his life as a recluse – spending his days and nights in prayer.[26]

NOTES:

[1] James A. Stewart, Invasion of Wales by the Spirit, p. 11.

[2] J. Edwin Orr, The Flaming Tongue, p. 1.

[3] James A. Stewart, The Invasion of Wales by the Spirit, p. 27.

[4] Ibid., pp. 28-29.

[5] T. Edwin Orr, The Flaming Tongue, p. 2.

[6] Ibid., p. 5.

[7] Ibid., p. 11.

[8] James A. Stewart, The Invasion of Wales by the Spirit, p. 17.

[9] Winkey Pratney, Revival, p. 177.

[10] J. Edwin Orr, The Flaming Tongue, p. 17.

[11] James A. Stewart, The Invasion of Wales by the Spirit, p. 49.

[12] Ibid., p. 51.

[13] Ibid., p. 61.

[14] J. Edwin Orr, The Flaming Tongue, p. 17.

[15] James A. Stewart, The Invasion of Wales by the Spirit, p. 57.

[16] Ibid., p. 39.

[17] J. Edwin Orr, The Flaming Tongue, p. 70.

[18] Ibid., pp. 70-90.

[19] Ibid., p. 80.

[20] Ibid., p. 102.

[21] Ibid., p. 107.

[22] James A. Stewart, The Invasion of Wales by the Spirit, p. 72.

[23] Winkey Pratney, Revival, p. 184.

[24] J. Edwin Orr, The Flaming Tongue, p. 23.

[25] Ibid., p. 24.

[26] Winkey Pratney, Revival, p. 185.

CONCLUSION

Bartlett quotes George Santayana as saying, "Those who cannot remember the past are condemned to repeat it,"[1] and Georg Wilhelm Friedrich Hegel as saying, "What experience and history teach is this – that people and governments never have learned anything from history, or acted on principles deduced from it."[2] Each of these quotes seems to refer to our downfalls and failures and doesn't seem to give us much hope for the future. God, however, in His Word seems more optimistic. He has actually written histories for our instruction, that we might learn from them! (Romans 15:4, 1 Corinthians 10:1-6, Hebrews 3:7-4:1, etc.)

If, we can learn from the positive experiences of history, maybe we can work toward the restoration of Biblical truth in our generation. For example, there is much to learn from past revivals: *How did they begin? Why did they end? What similarities can be found in each revival? What conclusions, if any, can offer insight and direction for our present situation?* While each move of God is unique and cannot be reproduced from a recipe, certain elements have been characteristic of all true revivals since Pentecost.

PRAYER

To begin with, every great revival in the history of the Church contains the element of prayer. On the day of Pentecost, we find the early disciples gathering in the upper room to pray. "These all continued with one accord in prayer and supplications." (Acts 1:14) The Bible doesn't record the exact words of their prayers, but we do know they were of one purpose and one mind. Why? Simply to receive the power and presence of the Holy Spirit that Jesus had promised prior to His ascension. (Acts 1:8) These men had already tried to stand in their own strength, when Jesus was arrested and crucified. Now, they knew the need for a visitation of God, if they were to fulfill the commission He had given them.

Throughout history, every revival of notable significance has been born through prayer. Whitefield and Edwards, the leading lights of the Great Awakening, were mighty men of prayer. The Great Revival, beginning in 1787, was preceded by intense prayer and fasting on behalf of many churches across the land. The 1857 Prayer Revival began as one man sought the Lord and encouraged others to join him.

Frank Beardsley, in his book, <u>A History of American Revivals</u>, states the following: "It is possible to have revivals without preaching, without churches, and without ministers, but without prayer a genuine revival is impossible."[3]

Revival author Fred Hoffman believes that prayer is not only necessary for revival, but that the Church has a responsibility to "pray down" revival upon a nation.[4] A key verse of scripture often cited in context with revival is II Chronicles 7:14.

If My people who are called by My name will humble themselves, and pray and seek My face, and turn from their wicked ways, then I will hear from heaven, and will forgive their sin and will heal their land.

Revival, as stated earlier, is primarily the work of restoring light and life back to the Church. Before a nation can be touched and changed, the Church must first come alive with the power and presence of Jesus Christ. "If My people" is a conditional clause, clearly stating that a choice of behavior is required on our behalf. If we humble ourselves; if we pray; if we seek His face – *then* He will hear and act. Before the Church can sincerely pray for revival, there must be a humbling of ourselves with sincere confession and repentance. It is not enough to just pray for revival, we must first of all see the overwhelming need for revival in our very own lives.

Men of old, such as Nehemiah, Isaiah, Daniel, and others, were willing to humble themselves and identify with the sins of the nation.

Knowing that – but for the grace of God – they were capable of the most hideous sins themselves, they gained a place of intercession before Him. Their humility, confession, and repentance unlocked the door for a move of the Spirit in their generation.

Like these men of the past, we must recognize that the Church is powerless apart from God and the work of His Spirit. Unless He sends a fresh outpouring of His grace upon us, our nation is destined for failure. Praying for revival, because it sounds like a good idea, will never bring revival. God responds to the desperate cry of His people. It is sincere prayer that moves the heart of God, and that kind of prayer is preceded by humility and repentance.

Another aspect of revival prayer is persistence. Men like Jonathan Edwards and Evan Roberts prayed for years, seeing little, if any change – until revival came. Most of us, on the other hand, find it difficult to pray for something for a week or a month or even several months before growing weary.

In 1984, I attended a conference in Alabama addressing the theme of revival. The purpose of the conference was to call the Church to prayer. Like many in attendance, my heart was stirred by the need for an awakening. Yet, in all honesty, I haven't been consistent in my prayers for revival. Again, we must realize that only God can put the burden in our hearts to pray night and day, week after week, month after month, until He makes the Church a praise in all the earth.[5] Realizing that we cannot even pray as we ought is a humbling experience. Yet, it is in that place of recognizing our need that true revival springs forth. If there is one ingredient necessary for ushering in revival, it must be the desperate and persistent cry of God's people.

One final point: Every good thing must come to an end – or so we are told. Yet, why do revivals often end so soon? One theory is that when revivals come, most Christians stop praying. The current awakening in Seoul, Korea may give credibility to this view. In 1960, an outpouring of the Holy Spirit began in Seoul that continues to grow into the 1990's. During the past thirty years, their commitment to prayer has increased rather than decreased. They believe that prayer is the fuel that has kept the fire burning.

THE WORK OF THE HOLY SPIRIT

The very essence of revival is a fresh outpouring of the Holy Spirit. The focus of our praying needs to be directed toward this very end. Jesus said that when the Holy Spirit comes, "He will convict the world of sin, and of righteousness, and of judgment." (John 16:8) Human beings are unable to convict the world of sin, of the need for righteousness, and of eternal judgment to come. That is the work of God and not man.

It is, in fact, the overwhelming presence of the Holy Spirit that distinguishes a revival from other religious movements or campaigns. For example, Charles Finney, often referred to as the "Father of Revival," may have had some insight. Everywhere he went, revival was said to follow. Was that really true? Yes, everywhere he went, people were gloriously saved. Hallelujah! You see, Finney realized that the Calvinistic theology being preached emphasized the sovereignty of God in an unbalanced manner. Divine election and man's inability to save himself, when preached in a Scriptural vacuum, leads to fatalism.

Finney, on the other hand, taught the balancing truth, that men were sinners by choice, and God commands them to repent and be saved.[6] For the first time, thousands heard the gospel in such a way that enabled them to respond to the message. Finney, of course, believed in the work of the Holy Spirit to reprove the world of sin, of righteousness, and of judgment. Yet a great measure of his success was based upon man's response to the gospel. Because evangelism is always an outgrowth of revival, everyone considered Finney a great revivalist. However, this author believes that Finney was a better evangelist than revivalist.

Evan Roberts, though, was quite the opposite. He prayed for thirteen years for revival to come – and when it did, Roberts took a back seat. In the Welsh Revival, thousands were saved, but not necessarily through powerful, eloquent preaching. More often than not, it was personal testimonies and the overwhelming presence of God that brought men to salvation.

What makes a revival different from any other spiritual movement? It's the power and presence of God, Himself. Men can create wonderful programs and even powerful methods of ministry – but it all pales in comparison to the work of God. Revival is the work of God. He is its author and finisher. While He allows us to participate in His work, apart from Him, there is no such thing as revival.

THE PROCLAMATION OF GOSPEL TRUTHS

Another commonly noted element of revival is the proclamation of Biblical truths. Every major revival has brought with it a restoration and proclamation of God's Word. For example, the Reformation restored the understanding that salvation is by faith alone and not according to our good works. Thousands were brought into a relationship with Jesus Christ as this message was preached across Europe. Wesley preached on the holiness of God and called men to live righteously before a Him. Not only was England delivered from spiritual darkness, but a new standard of integrity was born in the land. The 1857 Prayer Meeting Revival further revealed the priesthood of every believer, as lay people discovered that God could use them. Yet, most of all, the proclamation of simple, Biblical truths (such as man's need for salvation, the power of repentance, God's love for sinners, and the gift of eternal life) are related themes in every revival.

Powerful preaching has often been a key in igniting the fires of revival. George Whitefield preached with such an anointing that the most hardened sinner would be found weeping at his sermons. One man confessed that he came with a pocketful of stones to break Whitefield's head, while he preached. However, the sermon got the better of him and God broke his heart, instead.[7] Timothy Dwight, president of Yale College in 1795, disarmed the philosophy of skepticism through his earnest and logical preaching of the Scriptures. His proclamation of the Word of God paved the way for a powerful revival in the spring of 1802.[8]

Proclaiming Biblical truth has always been an important part of every revival. Whether it's through preaching, public testimony, one-on-one sharing, the distribution of tracts or the free use of the public press, the presentation of the gospel of Christ "is the power of God unto salvation for everyone who believes." (Romans 1:16) One thing is essential – the gospel must be preached!

For whoever calls upon the name of the Lord shall be saved. How then shall they call on Him in whom they have not believed? And how shall they believe in Him of whom they have not heard? And how shall they hear without a preacher. (Romans 10:13-14)

FOR THE FUTURE...

Though Hegel feels that no one ever learns from the past, I hope we can prove him wrong. As Thucydides said of his history, so I will say of this work:

... But I shall be content, if it is judged useful by those inquirers who desire an exact knowledge of the past as an aid to the interpretation of the future, which in the course of human things must resemble [the past] if it does not reflect [upon] it.[9]

Therefore, "reflect upon them" we must, asking, *"What insights can we gain from these revivals that may be relevant to us in this hour and beyond?"*

First of all, from studying the social conditions surrounding revivals, I can see that *revival is a gift of grace – in spite of man's rebellion.* The history of spiritual awakenings indicates that revival comes when conditions are at their worst. It comes, however, not because of those conditions, but because of the will of God. When the law is powerless to bring about change, God invades the atmosphere and rescues men from their own depravity. Revival cleanses the atmosphere like a summer shower.

In our locale, during the hot summer months, it is customary for the humidity to build until the atmosphere becomes unbearable. Finally, when the conditions are correct, the clouds release their moisture and we get rain – rain from heaven. Not only is the atmosphere cleansed and everyone refreshed, but the grass and trees wear a new, verdant hue. Everything looks crisp and fresh and life can proceed with a renewed sense of well-being. So it is with the great awakenings of history. Revival really is rain from heaven!

Secondly, through studying the history of the Church, I have become more fully aware of our acute need for revival. A dangerous combination exists in this country today: Evil is abounding in society and apathy is abounding in the Church. One of the grave dangers we face at present is being satisfied with our level of spirituality. Though progress is being made, apathy still clings to much of the Body of Christ. Spiritual lethargy has always been a deterrent to forward progress, deceiving us into accepting mediocrity as God's standard. We must not measure ourselves by the standards of the world – or pause too long to congratulate ourselves, because we are better than we were. Rather, we must evaluate ourselves according to the standard of God's Word. The Church is not operating in her fullness, until we look like Jesus on the earth. (Ephesians 4:13b) This is only possible through revival.

Finally, we must act upon our need. If revival is to come, we must truly humble ourselves and pray. We must thirst for Him as a deer pants for the water brook, (Psalms 42:1) and seek for Him as for silver and fine gold. (Proverbs 2:1-9) God has promised that He will "avenge His own elect who cry out day and night to Him." (Luke 18:7) The question is: *Are we willing to pay the price?*

Finally, my honest evaluation is this: We need another great revival, if America is to survive as a free nation and stronghold of evangelical faith. For this to happen, we must see our need for HIM, not just our need for power or prosperity or the things of God – or even for holiness or revival – but our need for GOD, HIMSELF.

As we pray, *"Oh, that you would rend the heavens! That you would come down!"* (Isaiah 64:1), I can hear Him answer, *"The effective, fervent prayer of a righteous man avails much."* (James 5:16b)

When He comes, we will be revived.

NOTES:

[1] John Bartlett, <u>Familiar Quotations</u>, 15th ed., p.703 #11 (Also see Euripides p. 77 #22).

[2] Ibid, p. 422 #9 (from Hegel's introduction to his <u>Philosophy of History</u>).

[3] Frank Greenville Beardsley, <u>A History of American Revivals</u>, p. 309.

[4] Fred W. Hoffman, <u>Revival Times in America</u>, p. 182.

[5] Note: the thought is taken from Isaiah 62:6- 7.

[6] Frank Greenville Beardsley, <u>A History of American Revivals</u>, p. 148-149.

[7] Winkie Pratney, <u>Revival</u>, p. 93.

[8] Frank Greenville Beardsley, <u>A History of American Revivals</u>, pp. 88-89.

[9] John Bartlett, <u>Familiar Quotations</u>, 15th ed., p.137 (Bartlett's quote from Hegel on Thucydides' <i>Historia.</i>)

BIBLIOGRAPHY

Ahrens, Herman C., Jr., ed. Christian History Magazine, Vols. II:2; III:1. Worcester, Pa.: Christian History Institute, 1983, 1984.

Anderson, Charles S. The Reformation ... Then and Now. Minneapolis, Minnesota: Augsburg Publishing House, 1966.

Bacon, Ernest W. Spurgeon, Heir of the Puritans. Grand Rapids, Michigan: William B. Eerdman Pub., 1968.

Bartlett, John, Familiar Quotations, 15th ed. Boston: Little, Brown and Co., 1980.

Beardsley, Frank Greenville. A History of American Revivals. New York: American Tract Society, 1904.

Belden, Albert W. George Whitefield - The Awakener. New York: The Macmillan Co., 1953.

Belloc, Hilaire. How the Reformation Happened. Dodd, Mead and Company, Inc., 1954.

Babington, J. A. The Reformation. London: Bradbury, Agnew and Co., Ltd., 1901.

Boles, John B. The Great Revival 1787-1805. Lexington, Kentucky: The University Press of Kentucky, 1972.

Bready, J. Wesley. England: Before and After Wesley. New York: Russell and Russell, 1938.

Buchan, James. Revival Fire in America. Unpublished research paper, 1973.

Cairns, Earle E. Christianity Through the Centuries. Grand Rapids, Michigan: Zondervan Publishing House, 1954.

Chadwick, Owen. The Reformation. Grand Rapids, Michigan: Wm. B. Eerdmans Publishing Co., 1966.

Cleveland, Catharine C. The Great Revival in the West, 1797-1805. Chicago: The University of Chicago Press, 1916.

Cross, Whitney R. The Burned Over District. New York: Harper Torchbooks, Harper and Row, 1950.

Dallimore, Arnold A. George Whitefield. Westcheser, Illinois: Cornerstone Books, 1979.

Davies, Rupert and Rupp, Gordon, general editors. A History of the Methodist Church in Great Britain, Vol. 1. London: Epworth Press, 1965.

Engel, Wilson, ed. Christian History Magazine, Vol. II:1. Worcester, Pennsylvania: Christian History Institute, 1983.

Fielding, Henry. An Enquiry into the Late Increase of Robbers. London: London Press, 1751.

Gallup, George Jr. The Search for America's Faith. New York: Abingdon Press, 1980.

Halevy, Elie. The Birth of Methodism in England. Chicago and London: University of Chicago Press, 1971.

Hoffman, Fred W. Revival Times in America. Boston: W.A. Wilde and Co. Publications, 1956.

Holy Bible, New King James Version. New York: Thomas Nelson, Inc., 1982.

Johnson, Charles A. The Frontier Camp Meeting. Dallas, Texas: Southern Methodist University Press, 1955.

Latouratte, Kenneth Scott. A History of Christianity, Vols. I and II. New York, San Francisco, London: Harper and Row, 1953.

Marshall, Peter and Manuel, David. The Light and the Glory. Old Tappan, New Jersey: Fleming H. Revell Co., 1977.

Maxson, Charles Hartshorn. The Great Awakening in the Middle Colonies. Gloucester, Mass.: Peter Smith, 1958.

McGiffert, Michael. Puritanism and the American Experience. Reading, Mass.: Addison-Wesley Publications, 1969.

McLoughlin, William G. Revivals, Awakenings and Reform. Chicago and London: The University of Chicago Press, 1978.

Moore, W. Carey, ed. Christian History Magazine, Vol I:1. Worcester, Pennsylvania: Christian History Institute, 1982.

Murphy, Owen. "When God Stepped Down from Heaven" (pamphlet).

The New Encyclopedia Britannica, 15th ed., Vol. XXIX. S. v. "Wars: United States." Chicago, Illinois: Britannica, Inc., 1990.

Olford, Stephen F. Lord, Open the Heavens. Wheaton, Illinois: Harold Shaw Publications, 1962.

Orr, J. Edwin. The Flaming Tongue. Chicago: Moody Press, 1973.

_____. The Fervent Prayer. Chicago: Moody Press, 1974.

Pollock, John. George Whitefield and the Great Awakening. Garden City, N.Y.: Doubleday and Co., Inc., 1972.

Pratney, Winkie. Revival. Springdale, Pa.: Whitaker House, 1983.

Roberts, Richard Owens. Revival. Wheaton, Illinois: Tyndale House, 1982.

Schaff, Philip. History of the Christian Church. Grand Rapids, Michigan: Wm. B. Eerdmans Publications, 1910.

Schmitt, Charles P. Root Out of a Dry Ground. Grand Rapids, Michigan: Fellowship Publications, 1979.

Smith, Timothy L. Revivalism and Social Reform. New York: Abingdon Press, 1957.

Stewart, James A. Invasion of Wales by the Spirit Through Evan Roberts. Ashville, N.C.: Revival Literature, 1963.

Thompson, Charles L. Times of Refreshing. Chicago: L.T. Palmer and Co., 1877.

Wallace, Arthur. Revival - The Rain from Heaven. Old Tappan, New Jersey: Fleming H. Revell Co., 1979.

Warner, Wellman J. The Wesleyan Movement in the Industrial Revolution. New York: Russell and Russell, 1930.

Webster, Noah (G. and C. Merriam, eds.). Webster's Third New International Dictionary. Springfield, Massachusetts: G. and C. Merriam Co., 1961.

Winslow, Ola Elizabeth. Jonathan Edwards. New York: The Macmillan Co., 1940.

ABOUT THE AUTHOR

Paul Moore and his wife, Myrna live in Clarksville, TN, where they pastor His Church, a house of prayer. They have spent the last thirty-five years ministering in the United States and in Europe – planting churches, praying for revival, and equipping the saints to do the same.

If you want to contact Paul, email him at HisChurch1@gmail.com.

59248331R00057